3/6

HOW TO SOLVE YOUR
INTERIOR
DESIGN
PROBLEMS

HOW TO SOLVE YOUR
INTERIOR DESIGN PROBLEMS

JILL BLAKE

HAMLYN

A Quarto Book

First published in Great Britain in 1986 by
Hamlyn Publishing
A division of The Hamlyn Publishing Group Limited
Bridge House, London Road,
Twickenham, Middlesex, England

ISBN 0 600 50302 X

This book was designed and produced by
Quarto Publishing Limited
6 Blundell Street
London N7 9BH

Senior Editor Jane Rollason
Art Editor Alex Arthur

Editors Emma Foa, Mary Lambert, Patricia Webster
Designers Paul Owens, Astrid Liberts

Illustrations by Ray Brown, Mulkern Rutherford Studios, Fraser Newman
Interior design plans by John Kempster, Greg Firth
Special photography by John Heseltine

Art Director Nigel Osborne
Editorial Director Jim Miles

Typeset at QV Typesetting Limited, London
Paste-up by Patrizio Semproni
Colour origination at Universal Colour Scanning, Hong Kong
Printed by Leefung Asco Printers Limited, Hong Kong

CONTENTS

INTRODUCTION

Whether your home is large or small, period or modern, in the country or in the city, getting the tone and style right is vital. Interior design and decoration is not just a question of choosing colour schemes, selecting different styles and ordering fabulous furnishings – it is about designing and decorating rooms so that they are practical as well as look good. It is about selecting schemes which enhance or complement the look and mood of the room. Above all, it is about creating a pleasant and satisfying living environment, tailored to meet your needs.

Most properties have their problems, whether structural or superficial. **How to Solve your Interior Design Problems** *offers advice on colour scheming, room planning, lighting, furniture and window dressing for every room. It shows you how to alter the shape and proportions of awkward rooms visually and how to enhance good features and disguise bad ones. Achieving the desired atmosphere involves careful planning but it is surprisingly easy to correct early mistakes, rescue a colour scheme which just doesn't work and even rectify a structural or design disaster. Simply adding, regrouping or highlighting well-judged accents and accessories can make a world of difference. There is also practical advice on choosing and using paint, wall coverings, floorings, tiles, fabrics and soft furnishings.*

How to Solve your Interior Design Problems is a practical manual manual - use it to help you plan new design schemes and to identify and deal with problem features. The book is divided into five sections. Section One - Design Analysis outlines the principles of interior design and should be used in conjunction with all the following sections. Section Two - Design in Practice deals with the specific interior design requirements of each room/area in the house, and with ways of lighting and window dressing in general. Section Three - Design Recovery offers practical solutions to in-built design problems, and covers renovating poor surfaces and disguising awkwardly shaped rooms. Section Four - A Sense of Style is an inspirational section, analysing the ingredients that make up popular styles, such as Country house/Rustic, Art Deco or High Tech. Section Five - Directory of Materials is a reference section showing in chart form all the available types of paint, fabric, wall covering, flooring and lighting fixture, and indicating their suitability for different interior design purposes.

The secret of design success lies in being able to look at the rooms in your home dispassionately and being able to decide whether you should throw out all the furniture and furnishings and start again or take what you already have and add to it. This book is designed to help you bring out the best in what you've got, with the hope that the many illustrations, descriptions and suggestions will inspire you to be a little bolder, more daring, perhaps even unconventional, in the way you fashion your home.

Jill Blake

Jill Blake
1986

SECTION ONE

DESIGN ANALYSIS

No successful planning, furnishing and interior design idea can exist in a vacuum, no colour scheme can be dreamed up in total isolation. Ideas have to relate to an actual room, taking into account its size, shape, aspect, atmosphere and positive and negative features. Its purpose and function have to be considered, together with the lifestyle of the people who use it.

Any good professional interior designer will spend time talking to clients to find out exactly what sort of scheme they require.

Professionals will often deliberate for a long time over personal design, and they know how hard it is to come to a well thought out final decision. A satisfied client is one who really enjoys living in his or her redesigned home. There is no point in creating a beautiful show house that no one wants to live in. The secret of successful interior design is to reconcile all the necessary items of furniture within the basic shell while creating a pleasing, harmonious environment.

Translating your ideas into reality can sometimes be the most difficult part of the design process, and it may only be possible to make final decisions, even decisions which alter the original plans, while work is in progress. You might discover structural problems and have to incorporate them. You might decide that the colour of the paint for the woodwork or walls is not the shade you intended. It is not until you start working on large areas that you can really see the overall effect. Remember, however, that rawly decorated walls, ceiling and woodwork can be transformed by the finishing touches of fabric, flooring and furniture. Maintaining a flexible approach to your design and making minor adjustments as you go along is one of the keys to success.

GETTING THE FRAMEWORK RIGHT

Think of a room as a basic box, however irregularly shaped, and break it down into its component parts. You will need to decide on suitable surface treatments and textures, as well as an overall colour scheme. Consider furniture and shelving or storage, any practical equipment like bathroom sanitary ware and kitchen units and appliances, window treatments and lighting and styling accessories.

ASSESS THE ROOM

Look at the room critically to assess its size and shape and any existing advantages it might have. Then consider any negative aspects or disadvantages. You should aim to capitalize on the good points, enhance the attractive features but play down weak points. However, if you cannot disguise obtrusive items, they can sometimes look better if you actually emphasize them.

ATMOSPHERE

Decide on the mood or atmosphere you want the room to have – warm, cool, elegant, spacious, intimate, stimulating, restful. The type of atmosphere you want will dictate the basic choice of colours.

STYLE

When thinking about style there are many possibilities to consider, ranging from cosy and rustic to elegantly traditional, extravagantly plush or minimally modern with all the styles in between. The style you select may depend on the intrinsic architectural quality of the building. It is safe to echo and enhance its natural character rather than try to disguise or compete with it.

The starting point for selecting a style may come from a cherished heirloom, a special collection of accessories or a particular design theme based on the pattern of a carpet, wall covering or furnishing fabric.

It does not take a design expert to give a dull box-like room character and atmosphere, but to match a good idea in theory with success in practice, you need to identify each aspect of a proposed design and understand how all the elements should come together.

Start a collection of samples, catalogues and pictures that reflect your ideal scheme or suggest different approaches to design for particular rooms. Do not buy materials or items of furniture at this stage.

BASIC PLAN

Work out a plan on paper. Whatever the purpose and function of the room, it will have to contain furniture. It may well need storage facilities and have to incorporate equipment and electrical and plumbing facilities. The way to work it all out to be sure everything will fit in and that you have the best possible arrangement is on an accurate squared-up scale plan (see page 12).

APPRAISE THE EFFECTS

Check your scheme out. Once you have an idea of the range of materials you might want to use, obtain larger samples and take them home. Look at

them in the actual room, both in the daylight and artificial light under which they will be seen. Floor coverings are seen both horizontally and from above and worktops are seen at waist level. Wall coverings and tiles are seen vertically both with the light shining directly on them and in shadow. An identical wall treatment can look totally different in two areas of the same room if the lighting conditions are varied.

USING EXPERT HELP
When you have planned the overall scheme and chosen materials you may have to call in expert help. The effect you want to achieve could involve new plumbing and electrical work, carpenters for fitting furniture or simply the aid of professional decorators. You might even need surveyors or architects if structural changes are involved. Get estimates from three or four specialists so you can compare prices and the amount of time the work is likely to take.

Scene change! The room before decorating (above left) looks smaller and darker, even though it is empty. Afterwards (above right) it looks much more spacious because a pale, yet warm colour scheme has been used. Pattern is restrained and textures are light but interesting. The furniture and furnishings are simple and streamlined.

If the first brush of colour or the first roll of wall covering looks stronger or darker, or paler than anticipated, don't panic. A room without the furniture, window treatment, flooring and accessories is only part of the total scheme, and will be transformed by the finishing touches. Check on colour matches as work progresses.

MEASURING UP

Before you can plan a room or fit in any furniture or appliances, you need to take accurate measurements. The most original design ideas can go wrong if the measurements are even fractionally out.

Measure everything and double-check your figures. Always use a rigid rule or steel tape and don't forget to take these with you to jot down measurements when you shop for new items.

Draw out a rough sketch of the basic shape of the room. Measure and mark in windows, doors, recesses and projections. Also mark in any fixed items, like radiators and heating ducts, power and electric points, telephone sockets, fitted furniture and plumbing pipes and outlets. Measure the width and height of door jambs, window frames and reveals, skirtings, cornices, coving, frieze (the height above the picture rail), and fireplaces.

CALCULATING DIMENSIONS

Work out the total floor or ceiling area by multiplying the length of the room by the width. Find out the total wall area by multiplying the length of each wall by the height, and adding them

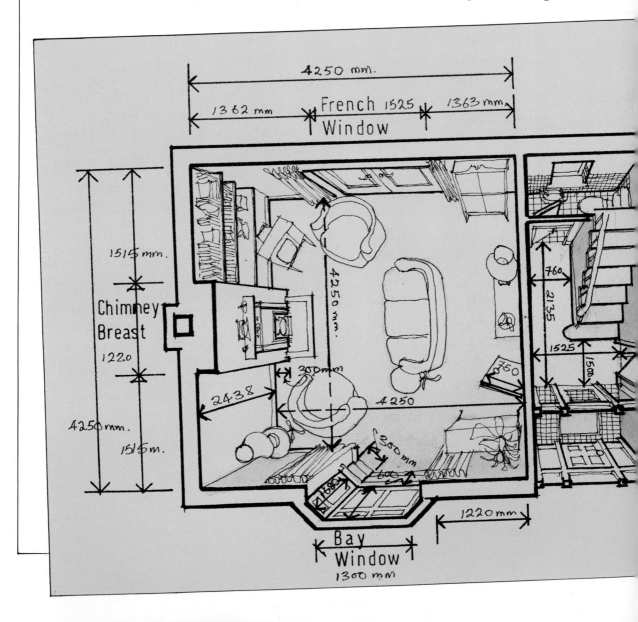

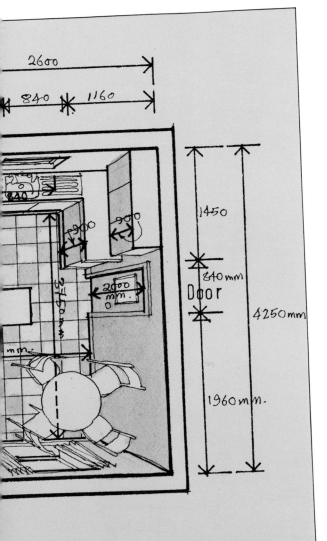

Before you can make a scaled plan to work out furniture positions and decide on any structural alterations, you need to measure everything accurately. Here the ground floor of a house with the 'lid off' shows the type of measurements to take. Don't forget to indicate which way doors and windows open, and to think three dimensionally and take height and depth measurements as well as width and length.

together. You will need these measurements to work out quantities of paint, wall coverings and floor coverings. You will also need accurate window measurements, as well as track or pole dimensions, and drop from track to floor and track to sill, to estimate curtain fabric requirements.

MAKING A SCALED PLAN

Transfer your rough sketch to a proper scaled plan. Work with squared or graph paper. A useful scale is 1cm – 25cm/½in – 12in ratio. Using a sharp pencil, draw the perimeter of the room. Indicate the doors, windows, fitted furniture or units, including which way they open, and all the other features to scale. Plot the exact positions of electrical and other points. Ink in the finished plan, leaving any existing fittings that you plan to change, for example bathroom sanitary ware, outlined in pencil only.

FITTING IN THE FURNITURE

Measure up accurately existing or new furniture, using a catalogue. Draw out the shapes on a separate piece of paper to the same scale as the room plan. Colour code them – and using one colour for existing items, and another for anticipated purchases – mark on them what they are and cut them out. This will enable you to try different plans and check that things fit.

When you have decided on the best positions for everything, tape the furniture cut-outs on to the plan. Allow enough space for people to walk round free-standing furniture, to push chairs back from tables and desks, to open doors and drawers and to pull beds out for making or cleaning underneath. The bathroom and kitchen are both areas where free access to fixed units must be carefully planned. Lighting and any plumbing changes can then be planned.

THINKING THREE-DIMENSIONALLY

It is often necessary to visualize rooms three-dimensionally. In the kitchen, for example, it is essential to see if work surfaces will fit under windows and whether appliances will fit under or on work tops. It may then be necessary to make elevated plans for each wall. Follow the same principles of measuring, squaring up and fitting in, with the shapes drawn and cut out to the same scale as the wall plan in elevation but showing profile instead of overall bulk. Tape the items in place once you have decided on the best position.

A three-dimensional sketch like this one (above) is particularly useful in kitchen planning as it draws attention to potential problem areas, such as surfaces that are too low for working at or sharp projecting corners of wall units.

When you are scheming a room, collect colour, pattern and texture samples and make up a colour board (right). Try to get actual samples, by writing to the manufacturer if necessary. If you are including patterned or multicoloured items, try to get a larger piece of the dominant colour. Add to your samples as the scheme develops and keep them with a list of accurate measurements.

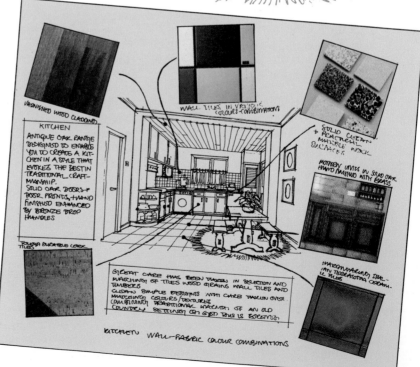

THE BASIC SHELL

Once you have ascertained that the floors, walls, ceilings and windows are basically sound, you will need to explore all the different materials and treatments available and select the ones which suit your style.

THE FLOOR

This is usually the largest single, unbroken area in a room, and although furniture will conceal it to some extent, it is still the most noticeable surface. Although the ceiling is the same size it does not have the same impact. Floor coverings and surface treatments, therefore, have to be selected carefully if they are to produce the right effect. There are four main types of floor treatment:

Hard floors are the most durable and are normally fitted on the subfloor. They stand up to heavy wear and tear and traffic. Some properties already have existing hard flooring, like floor boards, which can be refurbished if they are in good condition. All hard floors can be softened and accentuated with rugs or matting, so think carefully before covering them up with another floor covering.

Semi-hard floors are also hard-wearing but tend to be softer, springier surfaces. They are again usually placed on the subfloor, and can be plain or highlighted with soft furnishings.

Semi-soft floorings usually come in sheet form and may be stuck down or laid flat. They are fairly durable and normally thicker than semi-hard flooring, making them 'bouncy' underfoot. Vinyls and linoleums are good examples.

These types of floor are relatively easy to clean and maintain. You must think carefully when choosing your surface. It is totally impractical to lay fragile floorings in rooms which are heavy traffic areas, like the kitchen.

Soft floor coverings come in many types of material, shape and size and are frequently laid on top of one of the other three types of floor. Some cover the whole floor and are fully fitted, but others can be loose-laid. How long they will last and how easy they are to clean will depend on the type of soft floor covering chosen – the fibres from which it

Picking out mouldings, cornices, beading and covings in relief helps to emphasize them and looks more elegant than an all-white treatment. A subtle effect is created (below) using marbling on the walls and glazing and wiping on the cornice.

is made, the length of pile (if any) and in some cases, the type of backing.

THE CEILING

Often the ceiling of a room can appear too high (see page 150). One way to make it appear lower is by decorating it in a colour and texture similar to the floor. If a ceiling features decorative cornices, coverings and mouldings, or perhaps has attractive old beams, try to enhance or restore them. A light colour painted on the relief decoration with a darker colour on the background or ceiling 'bed' will help dramatize the effect of decorative plasterwork. Some ceilings may have been covered with textured paint or fitted with tiles. These surfaces often prove difficult to remove but it is worth persevering. Ceilings can also be clad in various ways to suit a scheme. You can use wood cladding, for example, and most of the treatments for walls are also suitable for ceilings, including tenting with fabric.

Think carefully before covering up a ceiling with acoustic or other ceiling tiles, texturing or cladding. Although effective, these treatments are not easy to remove when you want a change of scene.

THE WALLS

The walls form a large proportion of the total surface of a room. They can be used to form a backdrop to accessories or to serve a definite design function of their own. Coloured or patterned in different ways, they can visually change the proportions of an awkwardly-shaped room, or they can be treated to make a room appear larger or smaller.

You will need to select surface treatments and materials to create the right atmosphere and style for the room, at the same time considering other practical aspects. It makes sense to use washable or vinyl wall coverings or impervious ceramic tiles in bathrooms where there are problems of condensation or splashing, or in kitchens where grease and cooking smells are likely to linger. Tenting the kitchen walls and ceiling with fabric would just be highly impractical. But delicate, pretty decorations are fine for a living room or a bedroom.

There are three basic ways of treating walls, but there are many variations within each group:

The natural look

If the walls are stone, brick, slate or wood-panelled or rough plaster, they will evoke a certain style and atmosphere in a room. They may need cleaning, renovation and sealing. Smooth, plastered interior walls can be given a stone or brick surface for a more natural look, or existing plaster can be hacked off to expose the surface beneath.

Paint

Paint for walls is available in several textures, types and finishes and can be used decoratively in many different ways. Painting walls is simple and colours can easily be changed if necessary. There are also various ways of enhancing a painted surface: murals, wall patterns, *trompe l'oeil* effects, and the special painting techniques of marbling, rag-rolling, stippling and dragging. A stencilled detail or an appliqué addition, such as a border, can be used to highlight a focal point.

Paint is also used for woodwork and metalwork. These surfaces are often seen as a 'trim' to a room, and can be picked out in contrasting or neutral colours. Alternatively woodwork can be made unobtrusive by matching or toning it with the colour of the walls. Wood can also be stained and sealed, rather than painted or veneered and polished to blend with the furniture.

Wall coverings

Wall coverings are available in a wide variety of types from conventional wallpapers to cork and other tiles and fabrics. Some, such as textured wall coverings, more easily disguise a poor, badly plastered surface than others. Start with a good, smooth wall if you plan to use reflective or delicately textured wall coverings.

Some wall coverings, such as easy-peel wallpapers and vinyls, are very easy to hang and to remove. They can also be painted or papered over. Other types, such as ceramic tiles, heavy relief wall coverings and some wood cladding or laminated panels, are semi-permanent and may be difficult to remove. Think ahead about changes you might want to make next time around and allow for this when selecting the wall treatment.

FURNITURE

Whether free-standing or fitted, furniture must suit the style, purpose and function of a room. Again choose the actual surface of the furniture – natural wood, highly polished or inlaid wood, laminate or upholstery fabrics – with care, making sure it fits your needs. Size is just as important as style. Think spatially when buying or ordering furniture. Avoid crowding a small room with too many pieces. Put striking items in a large room or group them to make focal points. Take height into account – high-ceilinged rooms look good furnished with several tall pieces. You could use bureau book-cases or cabinets in a living room, for example, or have a dominating bedhead or four-poster bed in a bedroom. Use your plans to work out the right scale relationships.

ACCENTS AND ACCESSORIES

The accents and furnishing accessories which complete a scheme are all part of dressing the basic shell. They can add character and style to a room as well as bring a dull colour scheme to life, or provide the necessary link to the visual cohesion of a room.

Accessories are anything which embellishes a room, from pictures, prints and wall hangings to mirrors, displays of books and groups of houseplants. Glass, china and pottery and displays of colourful cushions can be added to living areas, cooking utensils to kitchens and linens and towels to bathrooms. Some people regard lighting as an accessory, but in fact it should be an integral part of the basic shell, whilst table and standard lamps, lampshades and fittings are accessories.

The moment of truth! Stripped walls, bare floorboards and uncurtained windows are easier to assess. You can see exactly how to improve or enhance the basic structure, and what visual tricks to play either to alter the size and shape of the room or to emphasize or disguise an integral feature like a fireplace or door.

You may have planned the colour scheme, selected patterns, texture and surface treatments, and decided on designs and furniture before the room was stripped back to the raw. Reconsider these plans carefully and be prepared to change them.

Any of the styles illustrated in Section 4 could be imposed on this room. You can be guided by the architectural features or you may choose to complete with them.

Ceiling
Consider: replastering or lining with paper; lighting (this is the time to dig out channels for wiring); retaining or removing cornices; decoration.

Walls
Consider: replastering of exposed brick and areas of poor plaster; wiring for sockets, wall lights and speakers; retaining or removing picture rail (perhaps with the cornices the effect is over- elaborate); lining walls before painting or papering with texture.

Windows
Consider: stripping back and sanding window frames; replacing stained glass in upper section; window treatments (maximize light coming into room by hanging curtains clear of glass).

Fireplace
Consider: excavating and installing a period or modern surround, depending on scheme.

Floor
Consider: refurbishing floorboards and replacing as necessary; sanding smooth, staining and sealing or covering.

COLOUR, PATTERN AND TEXTURE

Colour, pattern and texture are the surface elements of interior design which can be manipulated to produce different effects of space, scale and shape, whatever the basic structures of a room and its furnishings. The decisions you make, whether colours for walls and ceilings or textural details in small finishing touches, determine the impression created by the overall scheme.

These three surface qualities are closely linked. In decorating, you have to deal with texture - the smoothness of plastered walls is totally different from the feel of wooden window frames and doors. These qualities are absolutely basic, even if you do no more than paint the room with the simplest of colour schemes. But you can also choose to add pattern and texture, to emphasize or to disguise. Whether you employ paint, fabric, paper or solid materials to create an effect, every decision adds another element which plays an active part. Each choice may modify previous choices.

COLOUR
A basic approach

Any colour scheme needs to be related to a specific room - its purpose and function, the number and type of people who are going to use it and the mood and atmosphere you want to create in it. If you are working to a careful budget and have to incorporate existing items or forgo expensive decorating and finishing materials, you can still be inventive with the colour scheme.

The lighting, too, can work some miraculous colour changes, and be used to emphasize good features and play down unattractive ones. Methods and effects of lighting are discussed more fully on pages 97 to 101.

An eye for colour

Colour makes an immediate visual impact and creates mood. It is the first thing people notice about a room, although they may not consciously relate the atmosphere to the colour scheme. When visitors remark how warm, cosy, rich, inviting, cool, elegant, spacious or intimate a room is, the colours used are directly responsible for creating these impressions. In fact, colour is an illusion created by the way the eye receives and the brain interprets light. It is these illusory qualities that make colour such a useful design tool.

Think of sunlight - pure white light. Pass it through a prism, and you see the entire spectrum, all the colours of the rainbow. Every object we see has a surface composition which absorbs light and reflects back only part of the spectrum, so what we see as a red object is one which absorbs all the other colours and reflects back only the red light. This is why colours appear to change under different illumination.

The colours we see all around us can best be described in two categories: the colours of nature in the sky, flowers, foliage, animals and birds, and artificial colours, those in which synthetic pigments and dyes are used in special formulae to create paints, inks, fabric dyes and so forth. There

are literally thousands of possible colours and colour combinations in the decorator's palette.

Working with colour

To be able to work with colour creatively, it helps to understand a little about colour theory. One of the best ways of learning about it is by looking at a colour wheel (see page 20). The pigment and dye spectrum relates to the primary colours of red, yellow and blue - all the other colours originate from these three entirely pure colours. Red, yellow or blue cannot be mixed from any combination of pigments. By using two primary colours together you get a secondary colour. There are three secondaries, corresponding to the three primaries: orange (red and yellow), green (blue and yellow) and violet (red and blue). These six colours make up the basic spectrum. The primaries and

Colour creates atmosphere and mood — pattern sets the style of a room.

The exotic ethnic look in this sitting room (left) owes much to the rich red, green and gold colour scheme, as well as to the furniture, furnishings and wall-hanging. The striped wallpaper makes the fairly low ceiling appear higher and the stripes echoed on the sofa help to make the narrow end wall look wider. Furniture is grouped attractively to form a conversation area.

Bold accent colours (top) can transform a dull scheme or bring a neutral one to life. The simple addition of basic accessories can provide the much needed contrast or harmony.

Black and white (above) can provide a perfect background — a non-colour scheme which is easy to plan and comfortable to live with. Textures must be cleverly chosen to add interest, and lighting should be dramatic and flexible. Bold splashes of colour in accessories add the necessary accent and emphasis to the scheme.

secondaries can be divided into opposite pairs, called complementary colours: red and green, blue and orange, yellow and violet. Each pair demonstrates the strongest possible contrast between colours, since the secondary colour contains no trace of its complementary. If you stare at a strong colour fixedly for a few moments, then blink or look away, you will see the complementary colour as an after-image.

The colour wheel can be further subdivided into tertiary colours. These are made by mixing together equal parts of a primary colour and the secondary colour adjacent to it on the colour wheel, creating red-orange, yellow-orange, yellow-green, blue-green, blue-violet and red-violet. These are all pure colours and are called hues.

All the colours on one side of the wheel are warm colours – red-violet, red, red-orange, orange, yellow-orange, yellow and those on the other side are cool – green, blue-green, blue, blue-violet. All the warm colours are 'advancing' or dominant colours, that is, they appear to come towards you. Strong, warm colours used in a room can make it seem cosy and intimate, but if too many bright, advancing colours are used in a small room, the

effect can be claustrophobic or extremely garish. All the cool colours are 'receding' – they appear to go away from you. They can help to create an illusion of space, particularly if the pale tones of the colours are used. If equal quantities of a warm and cool colour are used together in a room, the warmer colour will appear to predominate. Two colours fall at the junction of cool and warm – yellow-green and violet. Their quality depends on their relationship to the warm or cool colour.

As well as tints and shades (see below) there are the neutrals. In interior design, these include the full range of grey, brown, beige, cream and off-white tones, but strictly speaking the only true neutrals are a pure grey, produced by mixing equal quantities of the three primary colours, or black and white together. All the other so-called neutrals relate back to the colours on the wheel: browns can tend towards red or green; grey can be grey-green, blue-grey or lilac-grey; beige can be tinged with pink, blue, yellow or green; and each tint in the entire range of off-whites has a starting point in the spectrum. This is why colour matching has to be done just as carefully with neutrals and pastels as with the bolder, brighter hues.

COLOUR WHEEL

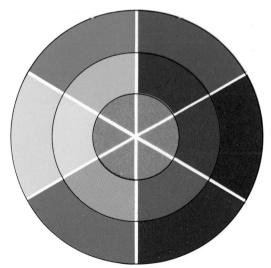

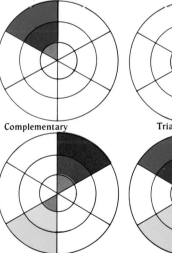

Monochromatic   Adjacent

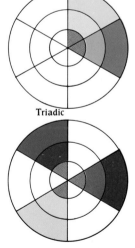

Complementary   Triadic

*The colour wheel shows pure hues on the outer edge — **primary** colours of red, yellow and blue, with **secondary** colours of orange, green and violet or purple. The middle circle shows **tints**, formed*

*by mixing these colours with white to make them lighter. The inner circle shows **shades** made by mixing black with the pure colour to darken and enrich. Basic colour schemes include:*

Monochromatic *— made by using shades, tints and pure hues of any one colour.* **Complementary** *— made by using two colours which face each other on the wheel.* **Adjacent** *— made by*

using three or four colours next to each other on the colour wheel. **Triadic** *— made by using three equidistant colours.*

Harmony and contrast

When it comes to planning colour for interior decoration, there are two basic types of scheme. One consists of harmonious or *related* colours and the other of contrasting or *complementary* colours.

A harmonious scheme uses adjacent colours on the wheel (sometimes called 'analogous' colours) or a monochromatic theme (tone on tone) using various values of the same colour, from light through to dark. Great care is needed when creating a monochromatic scheme to ensure noticeable contrast between the tones, or it may seem dull. The simplest monochrome range· is based on a single segment of the colour wheel. It is rarely successful to mix pure colours with secondaries and tertiaries made from the same colour. This requires good judgement for successful translation to a large scale.

Harmonious colour schemes are usually easy to live with and tend to create a relaxed atmosphere. They make a useful background for patterned furnishing fabrics, as they do not compete.

Contrasting or complementary schemes are created by using colours opposite each other on the wheel, for example, red with green or blue with orange. Contrasting colour schemes are more exciting than harmonious ones – they can be highly stimulating and are rarely restful.

A split-complementary scheme occurs when three colours equidistant on the wheel are combined – as with the three primaries of red, yellow and blue, or with red-orange, yellow-green and blue-violet. A scheme involving a fourth distinct hue is called a tetrad.

Colour theory helps to explain the behaviour of colour and the relationships of different hues. But there are modifying factors that must be used in your planning, when it comes to dealing with paint, fabric and paper, and with space, mass and light. The pigments and dyes that create the colours of different materials do not conform absolutely to the theory of colour. Some pigments, for example, are impure and devalue a colour mixture, while others dominate weaker colours. Black or strong red will flood out a paint mixture rather than enrich it. The same colour dyed into fabric and painted on the wall will have different qualities in each case. The colour of paint is modified by a gloss or matt finish and may alter as the paint dries. Here again, it is important to have samples of all the actual materials and to observe the effect *in situ.*

The warm colour scheme (top) is based on tones of rich reds, creams, browns and gold, and further enhanced by touches of brass and gilt. The blue accents emphasize the warmth of the rest of the room.

The cool colour scheme (above) is created by the bold use of blocks of cold colours — blues and greens, with neutral white. Warm golden lighting provides colour contrast.

Putting theory into practice

To translate your colour ideas into reality, start once again with the basic features of a room – its shape, size, and intrinsic atmosphere. Consider also the amount of natural daylight it receives. If a room is cold, you can use mainly warm colours. These can be light, dark, rich or strong, depending on the size of the room. If you want to make it seem more spacious, use pastel colours – pale pink, peach, apricot, pastel yellow, warm beige, cream. If it is a large room, it will support stronger values – pure red, orange and yellow. If it is dark as well as cold, create a sunny impression by using lots of yellow and yellow-orange teamed with sparkling white or vibrant orange, set off against a smooth cream.

If the room is warm and has plenty of light, it will look elegant decorated in the cooler colours – blue, green, lilac, blue-violet, cool grey and black and white. Again, if it is a large area, you can use stronger hues, but if it is small and you want to create an illusion of space, use the very palest values from the cool side of the wheel. A restrained, cool, monochromatic scheme creates the most spacious impression of all.

Many schemes benefit from some neutral touches, to act as a contrast or a link. Neutrals are often chosen for the ceiling or paintwork, as the background to the wall covering or fabric, or for the floor area, but neutrals need not be used in this way. They can play an integral part in the scheme – or be used to construct a whole scheme, creating a restrained, elegant atmosphere. In order to emphasize a scheme and highlight its basically warm or cool character, add a few contrasting accents from the opposite side of the colour wheel. Alternatively use accents for tonal contrast. If a room is decorated mainly in cool pale greens, add some rich terracotta or rose accents, or for a really vibrant effect, red or orange. If it is schemed in rich, dark blues, choose soft pink, peach, apricot, sunshine or primrose yellow. In a pastel pink or pale golden-yellow room, add some spice with strong lime or jade-green touches. Tone down a rich orange, brown or gold room with flashes of turquoise, mint green or periwinkle blue. If the scheme is basically neutral, perhaps based on black, white and grey – you can use strong, contrasting, warm accents – primary red, yellow or orange; or cool ones – emerald green, vivid blue-violet, peacock blue.

Another way to build up a scheme is by starting

1

2

3

4

Colour can be used to change the shape of a room as well as to create mood (left).

Paint a high ceiling a dark, strong, rich or bright colour to make it seem lower. If it is very high, echo the colour used on the floor (1). Horizontal stripes round a wall lower a high ceiling (2) — and vertical stripes make a room higher, but smaller (3). To make a room seem less long use a strong colour on opposite walls (4).

A patterned fabric can be a good starting point for a colour scheme. The walls, ceiling and woodwork (below) are all painted a soft, warm rose-apricot to link with the floral pattern on the sofas. The same colour is echoed in a deeper tone in the carpet and on plain cushions. The window is unusually shaped, and the pleated blinds do not detract from it. Touches of blue in the upholstery fabric and the green house plants, provide some cool, contrasting accents to help to emphasize the mainly warm colour scheme.

with a patterned fabric, floor covering or wall covering, which incorporates several colours. Identify the component colours in the fabric and perhaps use the background colour, particularly if it is neutral, for the ceiling and paintwork. Pick out a stronger colour for furniture or bedcovers and another for the windows. Choose a relatively bold or vibrant colour for accents and accessories.

Creating a mood

If you want to create a specific atmosphere or mood in a room, you do not necessarily have to consider its size, which direction it faces or whether it is dark or light. Concentrate solely on the colours which will create the required impression and rely on furnishings and finishing touches to expand the concept. Each colour has basic characteristics representing particular moods and associations, although of course response to colour is individual.

COLOUR MATCHING – THE PROFESSIONAL WAY

Colour matching can never be a hit or miss affair. The only way to get it right is by colour sampling — take material or paper examples of existing items with you when you shop for the rest of the scheme. Add samples as you go along, take them all back home and look at them in the actual environment in which they will be used and against daylight and artificial light.

Make a colour board from a piece of card and a stout clip to hold the samples and design information. Start with your scale plan and proposed furniture positions (see page 12), and your list of measurements. Add samples of existing items or colour-match to paint cards or chips. Build up the scheme as you go along, adding new samples.

Do some sketches of the room, using coloured overlays to outline the floor, wall or furniture colours. This is a particularly good idea if you are undecided about your scheme, and if you like two or three different wall coverings, carpets or fabrics. Make several colour boards or sketches and seek a second opinion.

Try to obtain large samples of material or paper which has very strong colour hues or is boldly patterned. A strong colour or bold design will be even more strident when seen over a large area. Buy small sample pots of paint to test the colour on an area of wall or piece of paper before making a decision.

Monochromatic schemes work well in a small space. This cold bathroom (left) is warmed up with a red scheme (below), sparked with touches of white. Gloss finish paint and strategically placed mirrors give reflected light and help to make the area appear larger, despite the bold colour scheme.

Red is the colour of vitality, energy and aggressiveness. It is bright, exciting and dramatic, but it can be overpowering and needs to be used with discretion. It is the strongest advancing colour, making a room seem small, inviting, stimulating. It can make you feel physically warm, a useful tip if you want to give a cold, clinical bathroom a warmer look. It is also an appetite-inducing colour – and hence many restaurants are decorated in tones of red.

As red becomes less intense, it becomes softer and more delicate. Rose and pastel pinks are often used to create romantic bedrooms, perhaps being considered too 'sweet' for communal living areas and unbusinesslike for work areas, although pink kitchens are currently fashionable.The deeper values of red – the rose, burgundy and plum tones – are rich and subtle. Their warmth and elegance can be used very effectively in traditional living rooms and large hallways.

In this simple bedroom, the furniture looks important (above left) because of the red bedcover and upholstery. In the second sketch (below left) the furniture fades into the background and the walls take over. Pink schemes are soft and romantic. Again these are based on tones of one colour. The plain-painted bedroom (above right) relies on textural contrast to provide interest. Accessories provide a soft touch (below right) — a simply draped table, a ruched, festooned blind and an attractive Art Deco lamp and shade.

Orange is very similar in character to red, and combines the physical energy of red with the intellectual associations of yellow. It is almost as dominant, intense and advancing as red, and can be used in much the same way. It will create a highly stimulating scheme, particularly if it is contrasted with a neutral or complementary colour. It is a good, busy colour for children's rooms, playrooms, bathrooms or any area where relaxation is not the main aim. When orange is lightened it becomes a peach or apricot tone and has a delicacy akin to that of the softer pinks. When it is darkened to deep terracotta, tan or brown it becomes very versatile as a decorating colour. These rich shades act as a foil for either warm or cool colours, and are effective when allowed to dominate a room, slightly accented with cream or white. Unlike the restless, vivid hues of bright orange, these velvety browns create a warm, relaxing atmosphere.

Yellow is a bright joyful colour, always reminiscent of sunshine. It is associated with the mind, intellect, creative energy and power. Bright yellows are strong and stimulating, bringing warmth and light into cold dark rooms. But the stimulus of yellow can also be disruptive, so use it with care. It makes an ideal focal point but needs plenty of neutral background to highlight it. Pale yellows are highly reflective and will make small, dark rooms seem larger and lighter. The darkened versions of yellow - mustard, gold and golden brown - have a subdued glow which is rich, warm and inviting. They are ideal for elegant, sophisticated schemes. When yellow tends towards green, such as golden olive, hues can look golden and interesting in daylight but appear dead, almost grey, in artificial light, so use with care.

Green is the colour of nature. It is refreshing and easy on the eye because it is a balanced colour falling between the naturally warm and cool ranges in the spectrum. Green tends to recede and creates an impression of space, particularly in its lighter values. It will bring a verdant, vibrant atmosphere into a dull town house or a flat without sun. The darker, richer versions of green also help to bring a garden atmosphere inside, but, as in nature, all greens gain clarity from a few contrasting accents. Grey-green tones are also affected by artificial light.

Yellow and gold are warm and welcoming — gold is simply a richer value of yellow, which has been mixed with black or grey to create a shade. Bright or pale yellow schemes will fill a room with sunshine as in the hall area (above), *and the lighting can be relatively simple. The richer golds used in this elegant dining room* (right) *need to be cleverly lit if they are not to look dull after dark.*

Green and blue are cool colours and will create an elegant and spacious effect if pale tints are used. Greens and neutrals in this hall (left) are used to full advantage to give an illusion of space and greater width to a narrow area, helped by the 'trompe l'oeil' painted pattern. Note the radiator colour, which fades it into the background. The mainly blue-green living area (below) is brought to life with some strong colourful warm touches in accessories. The bold blocks of colour help to emphasize the unusual ceiling and wall shape without making the angles too defined.

Blue is the colour of harmony and peace, also associated with steadfastness and loyalty. It is basically a cool colour, and particularly in its paler tints when it creates an impression of wide vistas and skies. But blue can be very demanding in a pure, strong form, so use it with care in confined areas. It can also appear much colder than green, so warm it up, if necessary, with definite contrasts. Blue will diffuse and soften bright sunlight, as it is fairly low in reflectional value, so it will calm down a room that takes the full glare of the sun. The greyed versions of blue can be rather dull unless plenty of contrasting neutral and warm colours are used to set them off.

Blue is used for a study area (below left) to create a calm, relaxed mood. Shelving can be painted to match a room scheme to make it less obvious, and appear as an integral part of the structure.

Violet, lilac and purple can be warm or cool depending on the amount of blue (cool) or red (warm) in them. The brighter, warmer versions of these colours can be highly stimulating and exciting (right) *but can equally well be used to give a serene atmosphere, particularly if contrasted with white or grey. Cool lilacs and violet are unusual but effective colours to use for a kitchen (below right). As hot, steamy activities go on in the kitchen and utility areas, cool colours are often a sensible choice.*

Violet is traditionally a powerful colour – the Imperial purple – and in its strongest tones is vibrant and demanding, sometimes overpowering. Use with care, especially on a large scale, and add plenty of contrast in a room scheme. A purple or violet on the blue side of the spectrum can appear cold, so treat it as blue; red-violet is warm and has many of the characteristics of red. Pastel versions such as pale lilac or mauve can be either warm or cold, and will be spacious or intimate depending on the amount of blue or red in the basic colour. Lilac is a romantic colour, ideal for a bedroom. The deeper, greyed 'plummy' tones of violet are rich, warm and mysterious.

Once you have decided on the mood you want to create and the basic colours, make a separate colour board for each room (see page 24). If you remain unsure about a scheme, or the decision is to be a shared one, you could prepare several alternative boards.

(see page 24)

COLOUR – IDEAS AND GUIDELINES

When you have studied the theory of colour and understand the basic relationships of colours, you can apply certain rules or break them with logical assessment of the likely effect. The following guidelines may be helpful.

1 Always relate the colour scheme to the actual room — consider the size, shape and aspect.
2 Use colour to help create mood and atmosphere — warm colours for an intimate, cosy effect and cool hues for a more spacious, elegant feel.
3 Decorate cold rooms in mainly warm colours such as red, orange and yellow, and warm rooms in cool colours such as blue, green and grey.
4 Introduce some sharp colour contrasts or accents to emphasize a scheme — light against dark, pure hues against devalued tones, warm colours against cool ones.
5 Decorate large rooms in stronger, richer or darker colours and bold patterns.
6 Use light, cool colours to make a small room seem more spacious and feature discreet patterns.
7 Use bright, advancing or contrasting colours to create a stimulating, active environment. Use pale, receding or neutral colours or a monochromatic scheme to suggest a relaxing atmosphere.
8 Consider the value of neutral colours as a link between pure hues or to tone down a strong, dominating scheme.

COLOUR PATTERN AND TEXTURE

PATTERN AND TEXTURE

Pattern and textural contrast and variety can be used to enhance the mood and atmosphere created by colour. A room composed entirely of plain surfaces may lack interest however good the colour scheme. The balance between the printed and actual surface textures in a room must be as carefully and skilfully selected as the colour scheme. Patterns and textures set the style of the room, whether it be modern, traditional, or one planned to evoke a specific period flavour.

Scale is an all-important element in the choice of patterns. The design should in each case relate to the size of the area over which it will be used. Nothing looks worse than wallpaper with an enormous pattern crammed on to small or heavily recessed walls, or walls peppered with tiny windows. This is especially true if the design has recognizable motifs – birds, flowers, trees or figures – that may be cut off at awkward points. The same principle should be applied to upholstery and soft furnishings. When covering a chair, for example, choose a pattern which successfully fills the shape of the chair back, seat or cushion. A bold pattern covering a small area of floor can make your every step uncertain; it may play optical tricks which are particularly unwelcome on a surface that should be seen as completely stable. Conversely, very small discreet patterns can make no impact at all if used over a large floor area.

Pattern tends to behave in the same way as colour. The bolder designs come towards you, and make the surface on which they are used look smaller. The simpler designs seem to recede creating an impression of more space. A boldly patterned surface often appears to be even more dominant than a strong, plain colour, particularly if it is multicoloured and includes strong, clear hues. A pale, patterned surface will usually be slightly more vibrant than a light, plain colour, but this depends upon the scale and colour balance of the pattern.

Patterns fall into many different categories, and within each division there is a good deal of variety. The following are the basic styles used in decorating materials.

Florals can be neat and pretty, country house chintzy, mini-print sprigged, full-blown or neatly regimented. Any of these styles may also be combined with stripes or other more formal patterning.

Geometrics range from classical architectural forms to vibrantly modern, unusual arrangements.

Abstracts sometimes suggest simple forms and shapes, but they can also make use of artistic techniques, such as the stippled surface of pointillism, the soft, blurred look of watercolour or the scribbled effect of crayon drawing.

Neutrals are the basic checks and stripes and woven effects, which perform the same function as neutral colours, acting as a break or link in a scheme, possibly bridging the gap between two different designs, or between patterned and plain surfaces.

Traditional designs are of various types which derive from existing and accepted styles such as

Classical, Georgian, Regency, Victorian, Edwardian, Art Nouveau, Art Deco and 1950s.

Ethnic patterns, such as Oriental, Asian, Indian, Mexican and Hawaiian, rely on cultural influences to form their style.

Picturesque patterns are highly representational, stimulating scenes or characters or posters. Many are designed for specific age groups, such as small children or teenagers.

Graphic or stylized patterns can also be highly representational, but are often abstract. Some are specially designed to simulate computer graphics.

Coordinated designs of decorating materials may be patterned in any of the design styles described

Pattern sets the style! Design contrast has been used in each of these rooms to achieve a pleasing balance of patterned, plain and interestingly textured surfaces, with entirely different results. The striped flooring on the raised bed area (below left) looks elegant, modern and geometric. The contrasting patterned fabrics in the living room (below) create a distinctly ethnic feel and the mainly plain bedroom (left) relies on the soft furnishings for pattern interest.

Patterns can work together successfully, even if they are not part of a coordinated collection. The secret is to mix like with like, or use a 'neutral' pattern like a check, trellis or stripe to link together two designs, or coordinate a pattern and a plain. Abstracts and simulations work well together (bottom left). Geometric patterns can be modern and graphic or classical and architectural (top left). Stripes, diamond trellis and chevron designs look good together against a marbled background (bottom right). Traditional Paisley, classic stripe and basketweave effect work well with a subtle pearlized plain (top right).

Pattern and texture interest can be restrained. In this room (above) the painted technique above the dado rail works well, when a strongly patterned wall treatment would be overpowering.

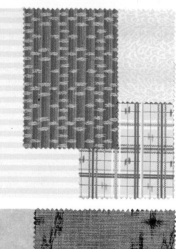

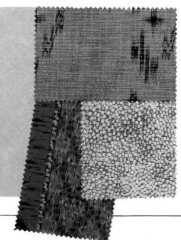

PATTERN - IDEAS AND GUIDELINES

1 Mix two of a kind — florals with florals, geometrics with geometrics. When mixing different types of pattern, create links between colours and basic shapes.
2 Use a neutral pattern with perhaps checks or stripes as a link or contrast.
3 Pay attention to scale — feature large patterns for big walls, floors and windows, and tiny patterns on small surfaces.
4 Mix patterned surfaces with plain to give high contrast and visual impact.
5 Strong designs will tend to come forward and make a room look smaller. Small or subtle patterns will fade away and make a room appear larger.
6 Choose the right type of design to suit the room style or to enhance furniture and furnishings. When choosing contrasts always try to see a large sample of patterned surfaces. Make sure they are stimulating rather than disturbing.
7 Put several plain items together, using the colours to create a patterned effect.
8 Introduce patterned accessories into a room where too many plain surfaces have created a dull appearance.

---

above, and are usually available as a range of different surface materials and products. Some ranges offer total coordination throughout the home, including curtains and upholstery, fabrics and trims, wall coverings, borders and friezes, bed linens, floor coverings, bathroom equipment and tiles, linens, kitchen products, blinds and many other accessories. To 'coordinate' does not necessarily mean to match – in fact to mix together is a better description. The patterns can be on a different scale but coordinated by shape and colour, for example, or the same scale and design on different types of fabric for different uses. Wall coverings may have two, three or four distinct but coordinating designs, with separate borders, suitable for all. Or the design may be repeated only in part or as a positive and negative version coordinated by the same colour or colour range. These materials have made pattern matching and colour scheming easier, and they can be used, in their different forms, on several surfaces of a room but they should be contrasted with some plain and some unusual textured surfaces. There may also be a paint range and some embossed materials which add these elements to the range.

A fully coordinated range can make a room appear surprisingly spacious, unless the design is very large or very brightly coloured. Many of the simpler, overall patterns with coordinated wallpaper and fabrics teamed with a plain carpet will make a room look cosy and inviting without decreasing its apparent size.

Making your own match

How can you successfully mix interesting patterns and textures in a room without being confined to a specially coordinated design range? The secret is to mix like with like, selecting patterns and colours which relate to one another in some elements. You may find this will mean selecting merchandise from the same manufacturer – most wall covering, fabric and flooring manufacturers work to a specific colour palette, certainly within each season, so many different designs will appear in the same colours or relate to a basic colour range. Mixing like with like means matching some elements of the patterns - putting two or three floral prints together, keeping a theme or particular colour range or using similar shapes of different sizes but the same basic proportions. Simple stripes, checks, weaves, trellis effects and heavily textured plains act as a link between two other patterns or may help to tone down a heavily patterned scheme. They can also be used very effectively to give life to a very plain room. Using the same pattern, or a very similar one, in varying sizes can work well, following the basic rule of relating the scale of the pattern to the scale of the surface on which it will be seen.

Imagining how a pattern will look on a large area can be difficult if you only have a small sample. The stronger patterns and the bolder colours seem more overpowering, and the simpler designs and pale colours tend to disappear, but it is often surprising to see how a pattern changes over a broad area. A roll of wallpaper or a width of fabric is at first seen on its own, but looks very different when it has the next length or width beside it. If you are planning to use a strong pattern, look at two rolls of wall covering placed side-by-side with edges aligned. Or look at two whole widths and the full drop of the fabric proposed for the curtains. Curtain fabrics are seen gathered or pleated, never perfectly flat, which can change the appearance of the pattern. Gather up a handful of fabric to see how it will appear when made up.

Items like ceramic wall and floor tiles can be equally deceptive. Select these from a stockist where you can see mounted display boards of wall

These traditional painting techniques (below) give an interesting texture to walls and woodwork — almost a raised or dimensional quality.

1 Sponging

2 Dragging

3 Ragging

4 Rag-rolling

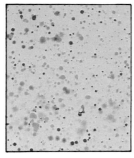

5 Spattering

6 Marbling

7 Marbling with jointing

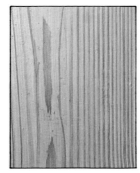

8 Wood graining

tiles, and where floor tiles can be placed in mirrored boxes, which magnify a square section of tiling almost to room size. If you cannot see the actual items scaled up in this way, there are special catalogues and leaflets designed to show an overall impression of the effect, although they are not necessarily accurate for colour-matching. Carpets and other floor coverings are sometimes hard to judge, especially if you are choosing a narrow width which will be seamed. Again try to see as large a piece as possible on the floor, ideally with two pieces side by side. Pictures in leaflets and catalogues can show you a more realistic effect and help you to reach a decision.

Patterning with plain

The simplest example of this concept is the way in which several different colours of plain floor tiles can be laid in a pattern – for example, stripes, diamonds or a chequerboard effect – or to outline specific objects. Plain wall tiles can be used in the same way. Two or three different coloured plain curtain fabrics can be seamed together into curtains or made up into a patchwork bedcover, creating patterning by simple means. Objects and accessories can be cleverly arranged – for example, coloured cushions on a bed, sofa or chair, or a variety of houseplants grouped together.

Another way of patterning is by using special painting techniques, such as dragging, rag-rolling or sponge-stippling, on walls and woodwork. The effects of some techniques are so subtle that they barely qualify as patterning, but they nevertheless create a more interesting surface texture than a completely flat coat of paint and contribute to a feeling of space, particularly in a small room.

Textural emphasis

Just as certain patterns create a sense of style, so do certain textures – some are frankly homespun, some are opulent and others can be starkly brutal. Hessian, canvas, leather, foil wall coverings, loosely-woven and open-weave fabrics suit a modern setting, while brass, velvet, satin and gilt may be more appropriate to a traditional setting. Ceramics and pottery, glass, brick, slate and wood will fit into many different styles.

Texture is linked inextricably with colour and light. Some surfaces absorb light, others bounce it back at you and these properties can make a colour look quite different, even if the same dye or pigment has been used. Shiny textures – gloss

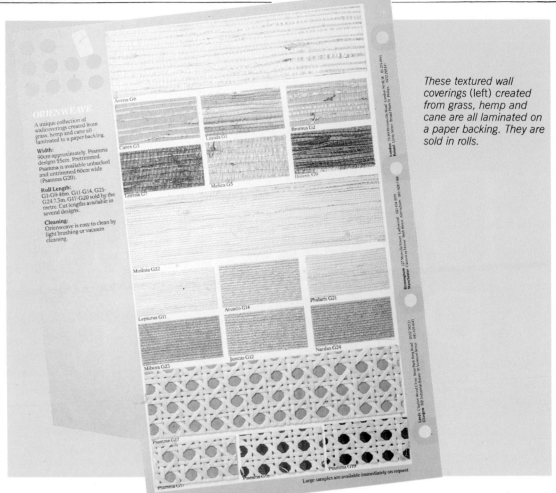

ORIENWEAVE

A unique collection of wallcoverings created from grass, hemp and cane all laminated to a paper backing.

Width:
90cm approximately. Psamma designs 55cm. Pretrimmed. Psamma is available unbacked and untrimmed 60cm wide (Psamma G20).

Roll Length:
G1-G9 46m. G11-G14, G21-G24 7.3m. G17-G20 sold by the metre. Cut lengths available in several designs.

Cleaning:
Orienweave is easy to clean by light brushing or vacuum cleaning.

These textured wall coverings (left) created from grass, hemp and cane are all laminated on a paper backing. They are sold in rolls.

TEXTURE – IDEAS AND GUIDELINES

1 Use different textures to emphasize a scheme and to contrast with each other.
2 Select surface textures that suit the overall furnishing and decorating style.
3 Make use of shiny or reflective surfaces to increase the apparent size of a small room. Work with matt, soft textures to make a large room seem smaller and more intimate.
4 Use a heavily textured material to hide a poor, uneven surface.
5 In a monochromatic scheme, make use of contrasting textures to enliven areas of plain colour.
6 Play off texture and pattern, using plain colours but noticeable textures to tone down a busy pattern.
7 Exploit the textural values of translucent or coarsely woven fabrics, allowing them to filter the natural or artificial light in a room.

paint, mirrors and mirror tiles, highly polished surfaces and glass – all reflect light to such an extent that they will increase the apparent size of the room. Very dull, matt textures – shaggy pile or nobbly-textured carpets, cork, tweed upholstery, flock wall coverings, velvet and towelling – have the opposite effect. They also help to absorb sound. Other textures – lace and open-weave fabrics, rattan and cane furniture, wrought iron tracery, trellised screens – all have qualities which allow the light to filter delicately through the material, rather than be absorbed or bounced back.

Take into account the quality of the surface before choosing a textured covering. Gloss paint, shiny foil wall coverings, silks and satins all show up any imperfections in a surface. Heavily textured, matt fabrics, wall coverings and floorings conceal uneven, dented or scratched surfaces, and thickly textured paints cover up surface damage on walls and ceilings.

SECTION TWO

DESIGN IN PRACTICE

Putting the design principles outlined in Section One into practice involves getting down to specifics.
Room-by-room design takes you through each room or area of your house or flat and illustrates in detail the stages of planning and design that will enable you to bring about the distinctive style and atmosphere you have chosen. For each room there are suggested approaches to the design, together with pointers on style, colour, surface treatments and lighting. The approach you choose will depend on several factors, including the space available and the main function of the room.

Whether you are planning wholesale refurbishment or making minor alterations, it is essential to consider the room as a complete entity and take into account style, atmosphere and function, together with existing decoration, architectural features including windows, and any furniture and furnishings you may already have. The initial step of deciding on a scheme can sometimes seem the most difficult to take, and looking at other people's interior design ideas can be a useful inspirational exercise. Flicking through the wide range of styles illustrated in Section Four of this book may prompt you to a decision. Interior design and home-making magazines are another rich source to plunder.

Tricks of the light emphasizes the importance of planning lighting at the initial stage of any new scheme and illustrates in detail how to achieve different lighting effects.

Ways with windows is a comprehensive guide to dressing all shapes and sizes of window. Several alternative dressings are suggested for each window type, so that you can select a style to blend in with your overall room scheme.

ROOM-BY-ROOM DESIGN

No two households have the same lifestyle or living requirements, and when you take over a new house or flat you may find problems that need immediate solutions. Assess each room or area individually, rather than tackling everything at once.

The best way to approach a difficult room is by making a list of the good features, faults and drawbacks, and if necessary measuring up and making a room plan to scale (see page 12). This is the moment to call in expert help for advice and estimates on any structural alterations.

If the area which needs changes is the bathroom or kitchen, you may well need to start by collecting literature on equipment, units, appliances and sanitary ware before you ask a kitchen planner, plumber or electrician round to discuss the necessary work. It always helps to have an idea of exactly what you want when replanning any room, but equally it is important to be flexible and to listen to the constructive suggestions of the expert. If the house seems to have several tricky structural problems, it is sensible to call in an architect or surveyor right at the initial planning stage. But don't forget that they don't have to live with the end result, so you need to know what you want and be able to brief them properly. If you don't like the plans and suggestions submitted by a professional, don't be afraid to say so, and try to work with him or her to achieve the right solution. Ask for a perspective drawing if you cannot visualize the plan.

Shortage of space or how best to utilize the space you have is a major problem in many homes. It may well be feasible to convert or extend the property but remember that a house which seems overcrowded with three or four active children or teenagers, will be more than adequate when one or more of the children leave home. In this type of situation it may be wiser to look at the house as a whole, and to re-think and re-plan the purpose and function of some of the rooms. Bedrooms do not always have to be upstairs, and living rooms do not always have to be downstairs. A downstairs room opening on to the garden can make an ideal playroom/ bedroom for two or more children. It may be possible to install a shower room somewhere or convert part of a bedroom to form a second bathroom to ease the morning rush. A garage which is not used much could be converted into a laundry and hobby room. If you have a loft, a conversion is well worth considering. It can be done on a reasonable budget and the extra room can be used as a living room, bedroom or playroom.

So getting to grips with problems comes down to tailoring your property to suit you and your family requirements, and decorating and furnishing it to give the greatest enjoyment to those who live in it.

ENTRANCE HALLS AND PORCHES

The visitor's first impression of a house comes from the front door and, if featured, the porch. If you have an older property, it may already have a very

Clever design and choice of colour can make a dreary 'tunnel' seem light, spacious and interesting. Good use of lighting and some 'trompe l'oeil' techniques have transformed the box-like square hall (above) into *an intriguing and almost theatrical setting. The grander, larger hall (right) has a warm, monochromatic scheme based on neutral colours, which are carried through into the other areas of the house.*

attractive front door which might just need a facelift. If the front door is unattractive, think very carefully about a replacement. Do not rush to buy a reproduction door unless it really does suit the style of the property. Sometimes an uninteresting front door can be vastly improved with new door fittings – handles, knobs, knocker and letter box – or with a different style of numbering or lettering.

If you have an open porch, it may be possible to glaze it to create a mini-conservatory or extra storage area. Bench-type seating with lift-up seats, for example, might be built into each side so that gum boots, shoes and other outdoor clothes can be stored. This idea is well worth considering if you live in a cold climate – the warmth of the hall is immediately increased as an airlock is formed. It is also possible to build on a porch but, as always, make sure it looks right with the architectural style of the property.

The hall provides an introduction to the interior decoration of the house and should have impact – it can be slightly more theatrical in style than other areas, and even a very small, poky hall can be treated dramatically. In some cases the hall, stairs and landing will need to bring together the different colour schemes and designs used in the various rooms, to create a feeling of harmony and continuity from area to area. Because halls are sometimes difficult to decorate, they may be redesigned less frequently than other rooms and decorated with a subtle patterned wall covering and in a neutral colour scheme. A hall, however,

should be designed and schemed with the same care, skill and flair as the main living areas. It needs the same considerations of style, atmosphere, size and shape. Above all, try to create an attractive, welcoming scheme and consider how the area looks when all the doors are left open.

Most halls do not actually need much planning and furnishing because they usually contain little furniture and few fittings, but if they are examined within the context of whole-house planning, it may be possible to utilize the space and to make the hall a dual-purpose area. A large, square hall can become a music room – if there is space for a piano or hi-fi system – with seating for conversation and listening. It may double up as a dining area. Fold away tables may be a practical solution here, perhaps with the stair well screened off by curtains or vertical or roman blinds. It might also be necessary to add an outer porch or install some inner screening to create a sense of intimacy in the dining area.

Space under the stairs can often be opened out to make a small home office or hobbies area or simply to form an alcove where an attractive piece of furniture can be displayed and dramatically lit. The alcove could also be filled with well-lit display shelves or used as a well-organized storage area. Alternatively, it might be converted into a small bathroom, lavatory or utility area.

If the hall is very small, you may be able to play some visual tricks to make it seem larger with mirrors and using a light colour scheme. The scheme will need to be very carefully planned, however, to accommodate stands for coats, umbrellas and possibly a telephone table. Sometimes a narrow storage cupboard can be built and the doors faced with a mirror. In a very limited space you may have to make an attractive feature of a hat-stand – bentwood circular ones take up less space – and an umbrella container, or fix wall-mounted storage high up if floor space is at a premium.

One way of creating more space is by taking down a wall or part of a wall between a very narrow hall and the downstairs rooms. Think very carefully before you do this and consider whether you really want to walk straight into the living room off the street. If an inner porch or some other form of screening can be installed, it will help cut draughts and provide privacy from callers. But it can still be an awkward arrangement and the heat loss will be considerable, especially if the area is open to the stairs. Inner walls between halls and living rooms are frequently load-bearing and a builder will have to help with any knocking down and strengthening.

The look

From a decorative point of view, making an entrance area work may well involve solving design problems. Hall, stair and landing areas often suffer from being awkwardly shaped – suggestions for solving some of these problems are given in other sections (see pages 130 and 146). An inviting, spacious-looking entrance hall with a well-coordinated colour scheme and attractive flooring is the ideal to aim for.

Style – the hall should have its own distinctive style, at the same time giving a glimpse of schemes to come in other rooms. It should also blend in with the architectural character of the property and be considered in relation to the exterior of the building.

If the hall is entered from a dreary corridor, box-like lift or directly off the street, it is worth creating immediate impact with perhaps a conservatory or hothouse full of luscious plants, or a warm and inviting modern or traditional interior. If the flat is in a well-designed block which has its own distinctive style, it may be better to echo the style, whether it has a period or ultra modern feel. In a house, let the basic character of the property take over. A country style, for example, works well in a country house or cottage, with quarry-tiled floor, arrangements of dried grasses, woven or wicker baskets and colourful flower displays. In a town house go for a more sophisticated look, perhaps with one or two elegant chairs and a series of prints.

Colour can be chosen to create warmth and space, and to give a cosy feel or a cool, elegant quality. Whether you opt for a more dramatic rich, dark, bright or complementary scheme, or for a pale, restrained one, use colours which link visually with the rooms leading off so that when doors are left open there is no clash. Modern houses sometimes run the same colour scheme throughout, perhaps picked out in the tiling in bathrooms, lavatories and kitchens or in the same carpet or floor treatment in the hall and main living areas. This produces a more streamlined effect and in a small house gives a feeling of greater space.

Areas of interest can be created with well-chosen furniture and accessories particularly if they are unusual or witty.

Take account particularly of how floor coverings look in relation to each other when doors are opened – and left open. Some halls can be used very effectively to display pictures, for example you can feature a mass of paintings and prints on one wall. Prints with coloured mounts can echo the colours used in other rooms as an additional means of achieving colour continuity. Other accessories can similarly be used as a link.

Surfaces will need to be practical, particularly in a house or flat where everything has to go through the hall. The hall, stairs and landing usually have to withstand much traffic, so floor coverings in particular should be good quality and hardwearing. A washable hall floor is the most practical surface if everything does have to be taken through, or in a very busy family situation where there might be several small children and dogs and cats. Tiles, cork, linoleum, rubber, cushioned or sheet vinyl floors can all be used. Stairs should also be well carpeted with a non-slippery surface. If the stairs are exposed wood they should be sealed, not polished, with a matt non-slip sealer. Floorboards, stripped and decorated with stain, paint or stencils, or with one of the specialist painting techniques, make a practical alternative to carpet.

Woodwork, particularly skirtings, doors and architraves, are subject to a lot of wear in the hall so a strong colour is worth considering as an alternative to white or a pale neutral. Stripping the wood back to the bare essentials and sealing or polishing it will provide an easy-care surface. Walls at the side of stairs should be washable .

Hall schemes are seen from upstairs too, so think how they will look through the bannisters and down the stairwell as here (above).

Choose any hall flooring with care — a patterned floor covering should link with the one used on the stairs. Think of scale and proportion — something which looks good on a large area of hall floor could look wrong on stairs and landing.

Think of the hall and landing floor in relation to the floorings in all the rooms leading off, to avoid a clash of colour or pattern. But don't play safe with a boring, plain carpet — go for something exciting in this area where you only pass through, and where a patterned surface is often more practical than a plain one.

Lighting needs to be fairly bright in the hall, stair and landing areas. Light the front porch or door area and control it with switches positioned inside and out. Light the hall or telephone table, mirror, coat storage area and cloakroom with good direct lighting, independently switched. Light the staircase so that the treads and risers are clearly defined. This may require several light fittings in a long run. Always have switches for these areas downstairs and upstairs. In very large houses, arrange the wiring so that all the lights can be switched on or off from the ground floor, and then from level to level.

KITCHENS

The kitchen is generally one of the most frequently used rooms, but often the most badly designed. It may simply be that the atmosphere is not right – this can be changed with new colour schemes, accessories and possibly a new range of units – but it may also be unsuitable for your requirements. Do not rush to rip out all the existing fittings, however, without thinking your new scheme through thoroughly on site. Sometimes it pays to live with mistakes until you are quite sure what your real needs are, and exactly what ought to be replaced and what can be retained. Over the years you will also find that your needs change with changing living patterns.

Kitchen manufacturers' brochures are not usually much help when it comes to good planning, providing a functional room and detailing how to fit everything you want into the space available. A pretty picture may help to stimulate ideas for style and colour schemes, but a kitchen in particular must be planned from a practical and functional point of view. To be able to work out just what you want and before you can brief a builder or professional planner, you need to understand the basic principles of kitchen planning, even if you are using experts.

Kitchen planning

Safety, efficiency and economy of movement are crucial in a kitchen. This means working out a sensible 'work triangle' within the available space. The shape of the kitchen will influence this area. There are some accepted layouts – the single line, the galley, the L-shape, the U-shape and the island (see page 44). Your basic kitchen shape and individual requirements may involve variations on these themes. The general aim is to reduce the amount of walking between food storage, food preparation and cooking areas – between the refrigerator, sink and work surfaces, and cooker. The ideal kitchen work triangle recommended should have sides of not less than 3.6 m/11¾ ft and not more than 6.6 m/21½ ft. Within this area there should ideally be no doors and the three points of the triangle can be linked by work surfaces forming food preparation, mixing and service zones (including dishwasher). Try not to site a cooker opposite the sink because of the danger of accidents when moving across the room with hot pans. Similarly a door should never cross the route from cooker to sink.

The kitchen should have as much style and atmosphere as any other room in the house, and basic interior design principles are followed when choosing the colour scheme and surface materials. All too often style is obscured by the practicalities of fitting in the necessary equipment and deciding on the appliances.

This rustic-style kitchen (left) could be installed in a town house, penthouse apartment or suburban property, to bring in a breath of country fresh air and inspire the most mundane of cooks.

THE KITCHEN WORK TRIANGLE

F-Shaped

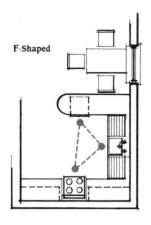

A fairly large kitchen can be divided into kitchen and dining areas, separated by a breakfast bar or peninsular unit (left and right). *Extra storage can be provided in ceiling-mounted cupboards above the peninsular unit. The work triangle fits neatly into the cooking/food preparation area. The serving area is practically sited near the table in this layout.*

U-Shaped

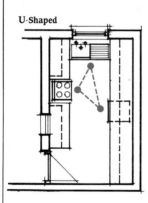

Long, narrow kitchens can have units, work surfaces and appliances fitted round three sides, if there is only one door to the room (left and right). *The work triangle should be kept as tight as possible. Don't site the cooker opposite the sink because of potential accidents with hot pans.*

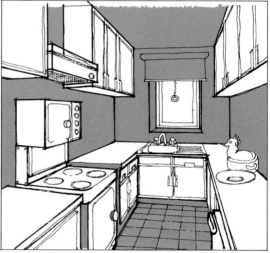

L-Shaped

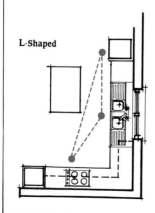

A large, square kitchen can have units and appliances round two sides, with a large multi-purpose table in the centre (left and right). *Avoid the temptation to extend the triangle too far — the distance between sink, food storage and preparation and cooker should be kept under 6m/20ft.*

A refrigerator or freezer is best positioned away from a cooker or boiler, even if they are well insulated, and there should be adequate work surfaces on both sides of the cooker. Group tall units – cooker housing, broom cupboards and storage cupboards – together, preferably at the end of a run of units. Never put a wall cupboard alone on a blank area of wall – try to site a unit, appliance or the sink beneath it. Do not be tempted, however, to put wall cupboards above or too close to cookers with eye-level grills.

Aim to zone the areas – utility, eating and working. The utility area will include washing machine, tumble drier, broom cupboard, possibly the central heating boiler, an extra (or the main) sink, equipment for ironing and storage for cleaning materials. Ideally this should be a separate part of the room, with a second sink used for food preparation. It may be possible to put the utility or laundry section into a separate room, for example, by converting an outside storeroom or part of a large bathroom. Every kitchen needs an eating area, however small – a pull-out worktop and stool can be enough for a snack meal. A good arrangement is a separate dining section with an extending table, divided from the rest of the kitchen by units opening both sides with a serving top. The working area is where you position the work triangle, and consists of food storage area, food preparation, cooking, serving, dishwashing and storage of crockery. To be realistic, the areas will overlap to some extent in most situations, and many of the surfaces will be dual purpose.

As well as fitting everything into the room, you will need to think three-dimensionally and make sure the units and work surfaces are comfortable to use. Site wall cupboards high enough above worktops so that you don't bump your head, but not so high that you can't reach things. Allow for units to fit under window sills, and place appliances like the dishwasher, washing machine, refrigerator or freezer under work surfaces, or alternatively to be stacked on top of each other.

Think carefully about the interior planning of units and cupboards – there are many types of interior storage fittings, such as pull-out sliding racks and baskets, carousel sections and paternoster circulating fittings, which help to keep everything clean, neat and tidy. You can also adapt other storage items for the interiors of kitchen cupboards and units – some office equipment, for example filing trays, can be very useful in the

When planning or installing a kitchen, consider safety aspects carefully. If small children are likely to be in the kitchen, fit child-proof controls and a guard rail around the burners. Keep a small fire extinguisher handy for dousing burning fat or electrical elements. Keep appliances out of reach of children and all wire and plugs well away from the water supply. Fit electrical sockets with safety shutters. Include more than enough sockets in your kitchen plan to avoid overloading adapter units.

kitchen. You may also be able to use the back of a door for hanging some small items, but be careful not to overload or the door may sag on its hinges.

Always consider lighting and electrical points at the initial planning stage, and have more than enough electrical points – you will always need double the number you first thought of. Alternatively, you could use a series of track systems which give a run of socket outlets along their length. Build in flexibility so that small appliances can be moved and plugged in at will. Light all surfaces well – sink, cooker and food preparation and dining areas in particular – and remember that although the sink may be under the window and well lit during the hours of daylight, it also needs lighting at night. Have the various zones separately lit and controlled, so that you can darken the working part of the room if you want to create an intimate atmosphere for dining.

Adequate ventilation is very important and needs to be thought about early on in relation to the position of the units and appliances – installation of ducting for air conditioning or the channelling of walls for power cables is semi-structural and should be done at the start. Cookers can be fitted with ductless hoods, which recirculate the air, removing smells but not humidity. A hood with a duct fitted to the outside will remove smells, humidity and a certain amount of heat. Fans set into the window or outside wall will remove the steamy vapours which cause condensation. Site a fan as high up as possible and as near to the cooker as you can. The correct size for your kitchen will be one which gives you 10 to 15 air changes per hour. Tumble driers require ventilation too, and most of them come with venting kits, but ideally they should be placed against an outside wall so they can be plumbed in to a proper ventilation duct. Oil and gas boilers, which are sometimes sited in the kitchen, need an independent air supply which is

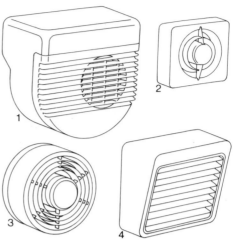

Kitchens, bathrooms and lavatories need 10-15 air changes per hour, so ventilation needs to be adequate (left). Slim-line extractor fan can be window or wall installed (1). In a larger bathroom fit a wall mounted ventilator which can also be connected to a ducting system in an enclosed space (2). Window fans can be circular or square, and have special draught stopping facilities (3) and some can also be adapted as wall fans (4).
In a square room (below left) a central island works well. A ventilation hood suspended above copes with cooking smells.
The conventional galley style layout (below) packs units and appliances round three sides of the room.

frequently provided by a balanced flue to the outside.

Heating the kitchen should be an integral part of the overall plan too, since a cold kitchen can cause condensation. The kitchen is usually heated by the same system as the rest of the house. Radiators from a central heating system usually provide adequate background heating, but it is useful to be able to give the temperature a boost. This can be provided by a wall-mounted infra-red heater, a wall-mounted or free-standing fan heater or a convector heater. If the central heating has not been extended into the kitchen, you can use oil-filled panel radiators which are plumbed into the electric power supply and are thermostatically controlled.

Before and after! The original kitchen (right) was little more than a scullery with cooking facilities. Now replanned (below), the atmosphere is cosy and countrified. The wooden units with wood worktops are echoed in the dresser-type, wall-mounted shelving. The walls are wood clad to match, and sealed with protective polyurethane varnish. A tiled panel above the work surfaces in the cooking and sink area copes with any splashes.

Following these basic principles of planning, you should be able to list your present and future requirements, leaving room for additions at a later stage. There is of course more to creating a kitchen than a workable plan. As with every other room, you will want to achieve a certain atmosphere, look and style, improve on any basic design faults and enhance good natural features. If the room is basically well-planned and attractive, you may only need to do a face-lift operation by re-decorating, tiling or perhaps adding new unit doors, to bring it up to your standards. If after considering all these points you decide you just do not have enough space, you may have to consider extending outwards or encroaching inwards, but again professional advice should be sought for any alteration as major as this.

Getting the kitchen installed once you know what you want can be done in several different ways. You can buy self-assembly units and basic appliances and install and decorate yourself or with the help of a carpenter. You can go to a builder, plan the kitchen together and supervise the installation. Self-assembly or rigid units may be used or they may be custom built to your requirements. Alternatively, there are specialists who can provide a total design service. Try interior design and/or architectural practices, specialist kitchen shops, the kitchen section of department stores or mail order. Specialists may quote for assembly-on-site, rigid (ready-assembled) or custom-built units, depending on your requirements. Some specialists will not undertake structural alterations, so you may need the services of a builder, electrician and plumber as well – and final decoration will probably be up to you.

The look

Apart from being workable, well-planned and equipped, you will want your kitchen to express your style and have some atmosphere as well. But in the kitchen, aesthetic and practical considerations must go hand in hand. You have to combine your stylistic ideas for an attractive kitchen with a plan including all utilitarian items.

Style – design the kitchen to suit yourself – country farmhouse, French Provençal, Spanish, streamlined Scandinavian, High tech, cosy cottage, exotic Oriental. There are as many possibilities as there are ways of cooking. You will need to select a

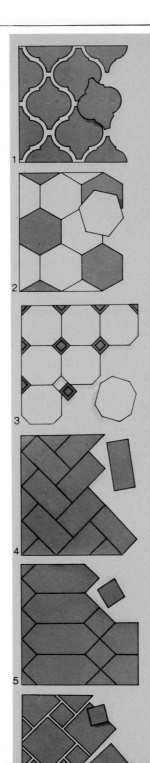

FLOOR TILES

Floor tiles come in a wide range of materials, including ceramic, cork, vinyl and lino. You can use individual tiles to form a definite pattern, and to create an illusion of width, length or space. Try light and dark colours, 'striped' across a narrow room or laid down the length of a squat one — or lay them diagonally corner-to-corner to expand the space visually.

Look at more unusual shapes, such as Provençal or Spanish (1) and hexagonal (2). Add interest to square ceramic tiles by choosing ones which have smaller, interlocking corners (3) which you can lay in interesting patterns — try a plain centre panel with bordered edges in a large room. Oblong tiles, brick pavers and woodblock tiles can be laid in a herringbone pattern (4) or can be mixed with squares to create an interesting design (5). Large and small squares can be laid to create a definite diagonal look (6).

style to suit the size and shape of the room though, for example, a country farmhouse kitchen with stripped pine dressers and a large scrubbed pine table in the centre will just not fit into a small room (for ideas see A Sense of Style, pages 158 to 175). You will need to choose units which are in keeping with the basic look – natural wood for the farmhouse, rustic or French Provençal, streamlined, bright units for a modern scheme.

Colour can be used to create the basic atmosphere. As most kitchens tend to be fairly hot and steamy, cool colour schemes can work well. Basic colour scheming rules apply just as much to kitchens as to other rooms in the house, so use paler colours and restrained pattern in a small room (see pages 152-3), but try some unusual colours, like a pretty pastel pink or cool, elegant grey. Accent colours can be extremely striking in accessories.

Surfaces in the kitchen in particular need to be practical. Although quarry tiles and flagstones create an authentic look on a country kitchen floor, they are hard on the feet and fatal to dropped crockery. They can be combined with strategically placed rush mats to counteract these problems. Quarry tiles are available in a variety of earth colours, including terracotta and mottled heather, and a variety of sizes. Cork and cushioned vinyls are warmer, easy to clean and bouncy underfoot. In large kitchens the dining area can have a carpet as a softer floor covering. Stripped and sealed floorboards are an excellent surface for a kitchen floor. Worktops can be tiled or covered with plastic laminate, wood or metal, depending on the unit type and the room style. But choose a work surface that is not too shiny, brightly-coloured or jazzy, otherwise it will soon become tiring on the eyes.

Walls can be finished in any number of ways, from wood cladding to paint or washable wallpaper. A matt finish for paint is more practical than gloss because a high shine attracts condensation. Similarly, ceramic tiles are not practical for all the walls if the kitchen tends to steam up, but they make ideal splash backs and focal points for the sink, worktops and cooker.

Window treatments should be simple and easy to clean, particularly for windows near the cooking area. Roller blinds are ideal and can easily be coordinated with wall treatments or used to create a splash of colour. Curtains will need to be washed fairly often, so the fabric should be colour fast.

1

2

3

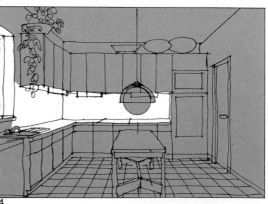

4

Venetian blinds are time consuming to clean, and are best kept away from the cooking area.

Lighting in the kitchen requires careful consideration at the planning stage. Light all the work surfaces, the sink and the cooker with good direct lighting. Fit any deep cupboards with a light, positioning the light switch on the door jamb so that the light comes on automatically when the door is opened. Light the table with direct but non-dazzling light, for example with a shaded lamp on a rise-and-fall fitting. In a large kitchen, fit some subdued background lighting or put the direct light on a dimmer switch.

Alternative kitchen lighting schemes are shown (left). *Fluorescent tube lighting beneath wall and ceiling mounted units* (1). *Individual spot and tube lighting positioned over work surfaces* (2). *Overhead lighting from a fluorescent tube combined with bright concealed lighting above cooker and surrounding work surfaces* (3). *Concealed lighting beneath run of units with the option of softer lighting over the table* (4).

Kitchen lighting should be as flexible as possible, providing both task and background lighting. Task lighting should be directed over the cooker, sink and food preparation areas, with softer, controllable lighting over any dining area (below), *separately switched, so that the cooking and washing up section of the room can be plunged into darkness while a meal is being enjoyed.*

BATHROOMS AND CLOAKROOMS

The bathroom is similar to the kitchen in many ways and shares some of the same problems – lack of space, lack of storage and outdated equipment.

Replanning a bathroom has to be done just as carefully and precisely as a kitchen, in order to site the sanitary ware in the best possible positions and to make any alterations to the plumbing relatively easy. As with the kitchen, even if you plan to call in the experts to re-plumb and re-fit, it does help to work out beforehand exactly what you want.

Above all, it should be planned for comfort. It should be warm in winter and cool in summer, and be functional without lacking personality. Everything should be positioned with practicality in mind – people need to be able to get in and out of the shower with ease, to kneel down beside a bath when coping with small children or be able to use the wash handbasin without bending double. They should also be able to sit comfortably on the lavatory or bidet and be able to reach towels or toilet rolls with ease. There are certain recommended measurements and distances to follow as a guide.

Bathroom planning

With the current fitness vogue, large bathrooms may well double as 'work-out' rooms, but even small bathrooms can have whirlpool massage baths, shower massages, saunas, jacuzzis, steam baths and other health aids. Baths come in a range of exotic shapes – circular, double-ended or designed to fit into a corner. Before you decide to put in one of these baths, check with a plumber that the boiler and hot water cylinder are large enough to cope with the increased demand for hot water and ask your builder to make sure the joists can cope with the extra weight.

If you have to fit in several new items, start with an accurate scale plan (see page 12). Draw in the existing items and superimpose the new ones. This will show how much of the plumbing needs to be changed, and how much room for improvement there is.

Bathroom fittings include a bath, an integral or separate shower, a single or double handbasin or vanity unit, lavatory and bidet. You may want to site the shower elsewhere in the house or flat to ease the morning and evening rush. It might be possible to install one in an understair cupboard, downstairs cloakroom, on the landing, or as part of a run of wardrobes in a bedroom or dressing area. It

When planning the bathroom it is essential to plan for people! It is no good fitting in all the equipment and then finding everything is too close together to be used comfortably. There are certain approved minimum measurements for user space of various items (below) — you need to be able to step in and out of the shower cubicle or bath for example.

Three possible bathroom layouts are shown here (below and right).
In the square room the recommended floor space 'mats' have had to be overlapped but the plan still works because of clever positioning. The bath in the square room can be stepped into from either side if necessary. The lavatory and bidet in the L-shaped room are sited in the alcove, and could even be screened off if preferred. In the long, narrow room the areas are zoned.

Square

L-shaped

Long and narrow

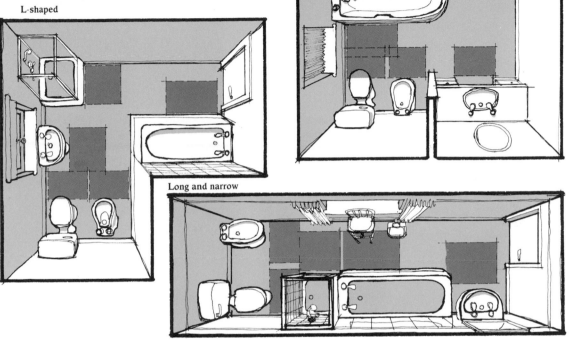

is still wise to include a separate one in the bathroom where it can be positioned over the bath. In a very small room, a ship's bath (sometimes called a 'sit bath') – the sort with a step in it which takes up much less space than a normal bath – might double as a shower tray and bath.

If you have a separate lavatory next to the bathroom, you may consider removing the wall to make a large room. Think carefully about this scheme, though, if it is the only lavatory in the house, as it might well cause problems when the bathroom is occupied.

Collect bathroom literature and catalogues and look at the type of sanitary ware available. Once you have some idea of the colour and style of equipment you would like to install, you can make a squared-up bathroom plan (see page 12). You will find that many bathroom manufacturers' catalogues include gridded paper for making plans and bath and basin shapes in plan form to the same

scale, so that you can move the shapes about on the room plan to determine the best position.

As with the kitchen, you need to think three-dimensionally and to make sure that basins, lavatories and bidets, for example, will fit under windows. Also allow enough space to accommodate the shower cubicle vertically. Plan in conjunction with the recommended measurements or distances.

Once you have an idea of what you want and where to put it, you can call in the plumber, builder or bathroom specialist. Obtain several different estimates for the work involved, and check the company's or individual's credentials with the association, federation or union to which the plumber or builder belongs. Also check whether the estimate includes the various sanitary ware fittings, taps or shower heads and whether the bathroom will be totally renovated and decorated. In some cases installation work is done, but the finishing touches are left up to you. If you are being quoted for plumbing with plastic piping as opposed to the traditional copper, it may make a vast difference to the cost. In some cases the traditional materials may be necessary if they are to be joined up with an old system or if period or reproduction items, where sizes can vary, are to be plumbed in.

Do not forget to plan the lighting at this stage. You will need to arrange for any installation of cable and wires before walls are tiled or decorated.

The look

The bathroom can be decorated in a number of ways. You can create a traditional bathroom including a bath complete with ball-and-claw feet,

high-level lavatory cistern with pull-chain, lavatory with wooden seat and a large-size basin set into a washstand top. Reproduction suites are available. Alternatively, you may want a Scandinavian bathroom, sauna-style with wood panelling throughout. Or possibly a bathroom which doubles as a modern gymnasium. Exercise machines, parallel bars, and a therapeutic massage bath can all be fitted.

Style will depend on the size and shape of the room, the effect you want to create, and the sanitary ware you already have or are planning to install. If the bathroom is used by a family, there may have to be some degree of compromise where

Bathrooms don't have to be cold, clinical and functional. They can be as pretty as any other room in the house. Some of the practical planning aspects have to be considered, but once the plumbing positions have been decided upon, you can let your imagination run riot.

The bathroom (left) is built into a spare room on a landing in a Victorian house — the double basins cope with the morning rush and the elegant ceiling is emphasized with a strong colour and decorative plaster arch and corbels.

The bathroom (above right) uses a warm colour scheme with white fittings. Tiles and paintwork in rich pink add a rosy glow.

The exotic conservatory-style bathroom (below right) has a real old bath complete with feet — the outside is painted a deep terracotta to link with the wall, wood and Oriental floor treatment. The garden room effect is further enhanced with plants and accessories.

interests conflict. When the bathroom is en suite with the main bedroom, it can echo the design and colour scheme used in that bedroom.

Colour schemes for bathrooms can be more exciting and adventurous than in rooms where you spend more time. Bathrooms tend to be a little cold and clinical, and a warm scheme may be a great improvement. If you want a quiet or neutral scheme, all the right colours to enable you to achieve the correct atmosphere are available in bathroom fittings, tiles and accessories. Cooperation between the manufacturers has ensured a good mix-and-match of accessories, such as blinds, shower curtains and towels. Several

BATHROOM FITTINGS

Fittings should be functional, but have style. Choose ones to suit both your bathroom and your budget. Try to plan ahead and think what your requirements are likely to be in two or three years time — bathrooms should not need refitting too often.

Basins come in all shapes and sizes and with or without pedestals. Choose a comfortable height for the majority of users in the family, and look for ease of cleaning and style

Lavatories should be comfortable and at the correct height for the users.

Baths are now part of the technological revolution, but decide on shape and size first before thinking about spa or whirlpool

extras. Showers can be sited in their own cabinet or over the bath. Bidets should be at the correct height for the users.

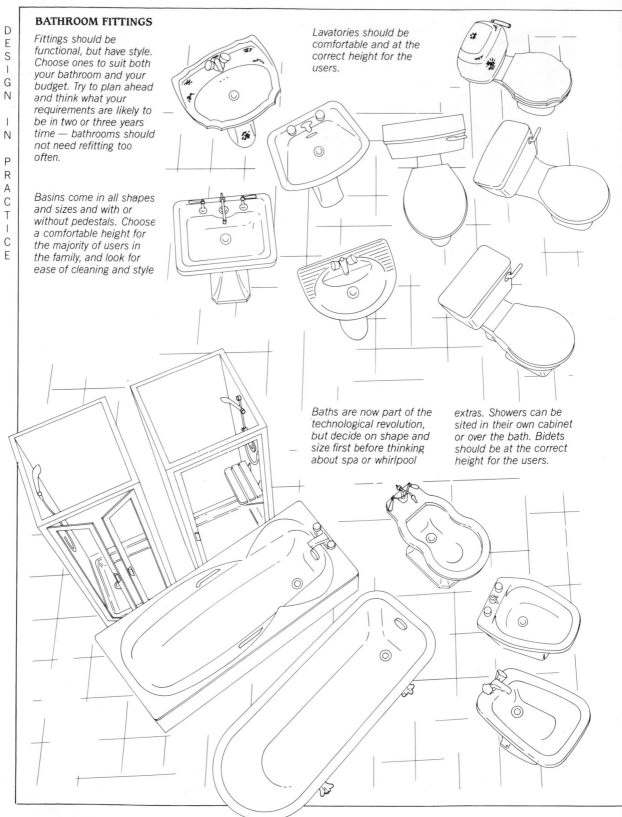

of the bathroom sanitary ware and tile manufacturers have combined to produce coordinated ranges, with recommendations in their catalogues. Always check colours in the store or showroom, however, rather than relying on printed brochures.

Surfaces need to be steam resistant, and if the room is prone to condensation problems, try to avoid too many shiny, cold surfaces. Washable wall coverings or matt or semi-matt paint can be combined with ceramic tiles. This makes a very flexible arrangement as you can change wall coverings or paint more frequently than you will want to change or cover up the tiles. If you do decide on ceramic tiled walls, make sure you know what they will look like over the entire wall area. One of the most successful ways of fixing tiles is to have part plain or textured tiles and part patterned, to form definite panels. Contrasting tiles can also be used in a border design to outline windows, baths, basins or other important features. Alternatively, use plain tiles set on the diagonal and edge with the same plain tiles set straight. This looks very effective with brilliant white tiles in a well-lit bathroom.

The bathroom floor is a very important surface – most people prefer a warm, soft floor covering but carpet is not always practical in a bathroom which is used by a large family. Properly sealed cork tiles or cushioned vinyl softened with washable cotton rugs are compromises. Carpet tiles are practical in a bathroom. Special bathroom carpets which wear well are also available. They are comparatively inexpensive and can actually be taken up and washed. They have a waterproof rubber backing and dry fast. Soft pile carpet is the ultimate luxury in bathrooms for adults only.

Lighting The basin, shaving and make-up area need good direct lighting, which shines on the face when seen in the mirror – the light fitting and mirror can be combined. Light the rest of the room with background lighting, with additional direct lighting for the bath, bidet and lavatory in a large bathroom. Make sure lighting is adequate in the shower, with direct lighting if it is in a separate cubicle. Light the inside of any deep cupboards. Make sure that all fittings are steam-, condensation- and splash-proof, and that main lights are controlled by pull-cord switches or switched from outside the room.

BATHROOM LIGHTING
Lighting in the bathroom should be efficient, safe and practical as well as helping to create the mood.

Fluorescent strip lighting (1, 2) comes in different sizes, often with built-in diffuser or pelmet. It provides clear light for making up and shaving, and is sometimes built into a mirror or wall-mounted cabinet. Theatre-style bulbs (3) can be used to frame a mirror or mounted along the top in a simple pine strip. Ceiling and wall mounted lights come in a range of shapes, sizes and fittings (4, 5, 7). A recessed downlighter, which fits into the ceiling (6) is another alternative.

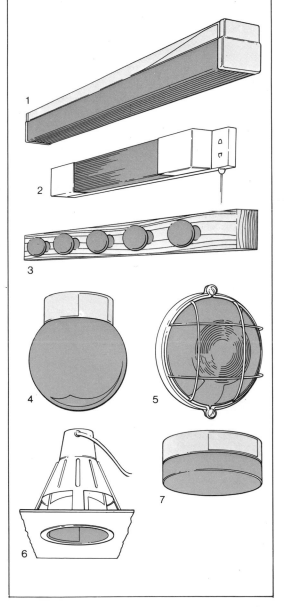

BATHROOM STORAGE

Units can be built in as in the dressing table counter (above right). *A tall cupboard in the bathroom which houses the water tank can be good for airing but not for continual storage as the warmth can rot fabrics and fibres. If there is space, balance it with a matching 'cold' cupboard. Don't underestimate the space under the bath. Boxed-in bath panels can sometimes be converted to open for storage. Some panels with their own integral compartments are available. Using the height above your head is not as common in bathrooms as kitchens, but units can be wall-mounted with strip lighting underneath to light a counter top, just as in the kitchen. Make sure they are high enough to avoid heads continually being bruised!*

Cupboards can also be ceiling-mounted, perhaps over a bath to form an alcove, with track for shower curtains.

In a large bathroom make an alcove for the bath by positioning tall cupboards to each side and linking top cupboards above.

Simple storage ideas also work well in the bathroom — a seat at the end of the bath with lift-up top, a towelling-covered ottoman with lift-up top or wire racks and stackable storage behind a roller blind. Alternatively expose storage to view in a minimally furnished room. A series of stepped boxes (above left) hold spare towels, cosmetic clutter and bathtime necessities.

Plants usually thrive in bathrooms, particularly steam-loving varieties. They can be displayed and illuminated in many ways, for example across a window on glass shelves (left). Climbing plants, growing down or up, can form a screen, either to divide off part of the bathroom or as a window treatment.

Taps

Mixer taps can either have a fixed position spout (1) or a swivel spout (2). A three-piece basin mixer (3) has taps detached from the spout. Pillar taps (4) have a streamlined shape. Old-fashioned brass taps have been adapted to a mixer design (5). Ornate ceramic fitments are another option (6).

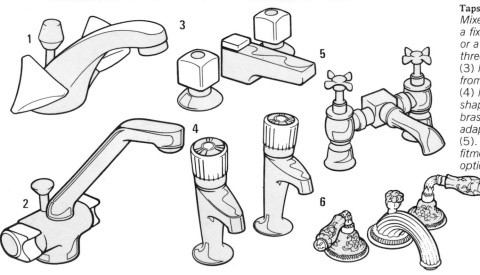

LIVING AND DINING ROOMS

Living rooms in family homes have lately become more formal in style, and the kitchen has evolved as the main family room, or the dining room has become a dual-purpose family and eating area, with the living room being used for leisure and entertaining. Sometimes it may be used just by the adults with the children using a more casual recreation room. If so, the furniture and furnishings can be much more expensive, elegant and fragile.

Furniture and furnishing styles have changed too – upholstered furniture, in particular, has acquired a completely new image, with much better, interesting and more comfortable designs, often replacing the conventional three-piece suite of one sofa and two armchairs. Many styles will fit into a variety of rooms and furnishing schemes, giving greater flexibility. Some special items of living room furniture in upholstered or cabinet style are almost an art form in themselves and can be used like a piece of sculpture, highlighted with angled spotlights. They can provide a dramatic focal point and set the style of a room.

Living rooms often need to be dual-purpose and to permit a range of activities. This will mean very careful planning to create a comfortable and inviting room, at the same time accommodating the different functions.

Dining rooms are a different concept, because they have to contain certain items, such as a dining table, chairs and some storage facilities. They can be formal in style, used only for entertaining and special occasions, or they may well be dual-purpose, with fold-away furniture, or include items which will perform several functions. Sometimes living and dining rooms are combined in one main living area. Two styles can be juxtaposed here as long as they are complementary or one style adopted throughout.

Planning living rooms

Your basic plan will depend on whether you are furnishing for the long term or whether you want a quick face-lift. It will also depend on whether there are any major or minor design faults which need improving. It pays to get the living room right at the start – if you have a comfortable, attractive room in which to relax and entertain, coping with other problem areas will be easier.

Look at the room and its basic shape, and decide whether you are going to make any structural

Living rooms need to be multi-purpose, and fitting in all the furniture has to be cleverly planned within the constraints of the room shape and size.

Always try to zone the areas, so that the dining function is separated from sitting, listening, television or study areas.

Long and narrow

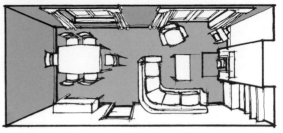

L-shaped

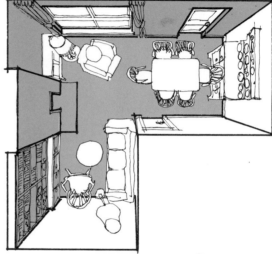

Square

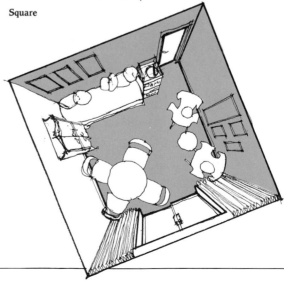

The curved shape of the seating units (left) adds interest to a long, narrow room, and forms a natural divider. Recesses to each side of the fireplace are fully utilized and the dining area is flexibly furnished to provide extra space when needed.

The L-shaped room is furnished in traditional style (left) so that the short, narrow part is used for dining and the major section becomes the sitting and conversation area. There is no need to emphasize the natural division created by the shape.

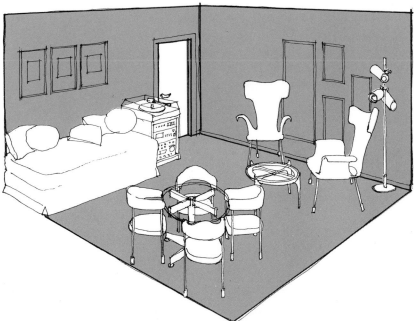

Square-shaped rooms are harder to handle as by their very nature they can appear box-like and boring. A very small room has been adapted for sitting and dining (left). The table with four chairs grouped around it takes up one corner in front of the window. This furniture is light enough to be moved into another part of the house if the extra space is required for informal entertaining.

Clever planning visually adjusts the proportions of this long narrow room (left and above). *The room has been zoned, with one end used for sitting and the other for dining. The sofa and chairs are grouped round a coffee table, positioned in front of the fireplace, and the dining chairs and table are sited under the window. The bold blocks of black furniture help to foreshorten the room visually. The neutral colour scheme helps to emphasize the beautifully shaped windows, which are left unadorned.*

changes, such as opening up or removing a fireplace, altering a window or possibly restoring original features, including rebuilding walls. In some large living rooms two doors can be irritating, so decide which one to use. The second door can be removed and the wall made flush on the living area side, creating a larger wall space. The other side might be converted into recessed shelving.

Once you have considered improvements, you will need to plan the various areas and activities into which the room may have to be divided. The sitting area will be the most important. Plan this first for comfort and flexibility. The conventional sofa and armchairs may not suit your particular requirements or room shape. Unit seating, individual chairs or two different-sized sofas are all possible alternatives. A conversation pit is worth thinking about if you are designing a modern room. Unusual pieces of furniture can be unified by their upholstery or by the clever use of colour and accessories. In modern rooms, all or some of the seating may be provided by floor cushions.

The sitting area has to be functional too and to allow for watching television, listening to music, reading or talking. This may mean that some of the furniture needs to be easy to move around. Always try to zone the areas in a living room, particularly if it has to accommodate several activities, and keep the sitting areas away from the main 'traffic' routes.

Make sure the items necessary for enjoying the room are stored in a practical and pleasing way. Books always look attractive on open shelves, but items like records, cassettes and video tapes are safer concealed behind doors.

If the dining area is part of the same room, but you do not want it to be too obvious, then look for practical furniture which folds down. For a room with a very limited space, a table which pulls out from a piece of storage equipment or one which folds back flat against the wall may be the perfect answer. Dining chairs can also be dual-purpose – they can be used as desk chairs, kept in the hall, be stackable or even folding and wall-hanging.

Storage items, such as glasses and cutlery, could well double up with the drinks storage unit – and this can make an ideal room divider, positioned to back the seating in the sitting area, facing the dining table. Zoning the areas visually in this way is very simple – there are other slightly more unusual ways. You can build a platform and raise the dining area slightly, sink the sitting area into a conversation pit, or go in for semi-permanent room dividers such as vertical louvre blinds, screens, folding doors or curtains. A change of floor covering – rugs, carpet or tiles laid to outline features, or featuring a border effect – can also help create a feeling of separate entities, without making the area seem cramped.

Lighting for living and dining areas needs to be flexible and functional, so part of the room can be 'darkened out' when not in use and so that various tasks can continue with the rest of the room bathed in a glow of background lighting. Also remember to install the necessary cables and fittings when doing any structural or preparation work, before redecorating.

In the living room, in particular, since you are likely to want to sit and relax, you should try to remove or disguise any irritating features. If it has a long blank wall, an unattractive window, or several different shaped ones on one wall, an ugly fireplace or radiator, plan to disguise or possibly to remove them before redecoration.

Divide and rule can often be the answer for a long living area! Open-plan shelves (1) make a good semi-permanent division, and can be used for display or storage. Folding or sliding screens (2), louvred or rattan, can look more elegant than heavy conventional folding doors. Curtains (3) are a softer alternative. They are seen from both sides, so a sheer fabric or double thickness should be used. If you want to open up the area occasionally, choose a retractable system, like blinds (4). Horizontal venetian or roller blinds have to be ceiling-mounted. These types of blind should not be too wide, so two or three may be necessary.

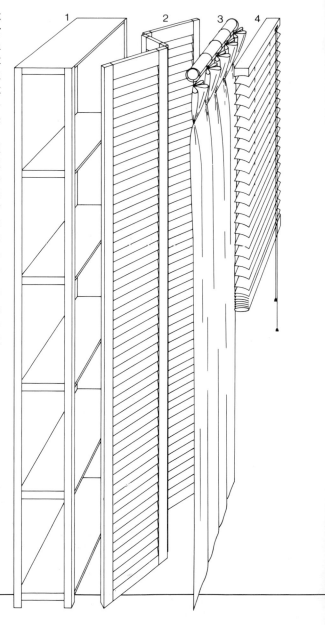

The folding doors (left) are coloured to match the walls so they fade reasonably well into the background — this type of divider should never be too obtrusive.

Delicate louvred screens separate a sitting and dining area for formal entertaining (below) and are also used to screen the window, creating visual symmetry. In a very long room, it helps to colour a divider to match the treatment used for the two narrow end walls, or windows as here.

Planning dining rooms

If the dining room is a separate room and you already have plenty of space in the house, then you will be able to plan it for formal and informal dining. In many properties, however, the dining room does have to be dual-purpose, sometimes doubling up as a spare bedroom, study, office or workroom, which may make a very formal scheme impossible.

Planning a dining room is like planning a kitchen – it comes down to the eating patterns of the household. If you always eat together but generally gather round the kitchen table, you will occasionally want to have a more formal meal. If you have a family, the age and interests of the children will also influence planning – very small children need very different dining facilities from teenagers. The type of entertaining you do, whether for friends or business colleagues, may influence the way the dining room is planned and styled.

If you are undecided about a plan or scheme for the dining area, think about your favourite restaurant and try to analyse its atmosphere. See if you can recreate some of that feeling in your own home. One important thing to learn from a restaurant is the use of subtle lighting and how to create an intimate atmosphere. Remember, however, that waiters are trained to skirt round tables and chairs. In the home you may well need much more space to circulate, to allow for chairs to be pulled away from the wall or table and for doors or drawers to be opened or closed.

Dining rooms and dining areas should be planned in practical proximity to the kitchen, possibly with hatchway facilities when they are next door to each other. If this is not feasible, then a heated serving trolley may be a good buy.

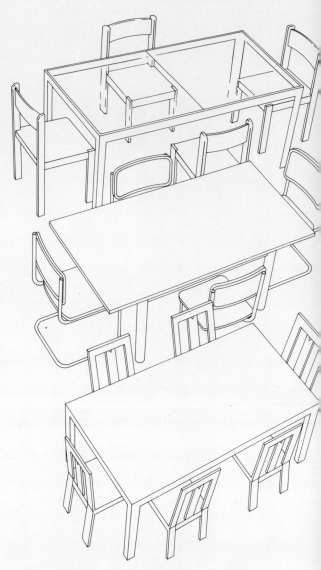

The look

The style, colour and atmosphere of the living and dining room/area will entirely depend on the architectural style, the size and shape of the room, the type of furniture you want to use and your lifestyle. All the different styles discussed on pages 158 to 176 can be used successfully in the main living or dining area of the home.

Surfaces can also be much more flexible, depending on the type of room and the use it will get. Obviously a sitting room used by adults only can be designed to have pale carpets, fragile furnishings and beautifully textured walls, but a living room for a family with pets needs more practical and long-lasting surfaces, particularly the floor covering and upholstery. In this type of combined living/dining area, a washable floor covering, laid throughout with a large rug to soften the sitting area, is a practical compromise.

Lighting should be flexible in living/dining areas to allow for different activities. Have background lighting controlled by dimmer switches. Good background lighting for living areas can sometimes be provided by highlighting various decorative items or illuminating display shelves.

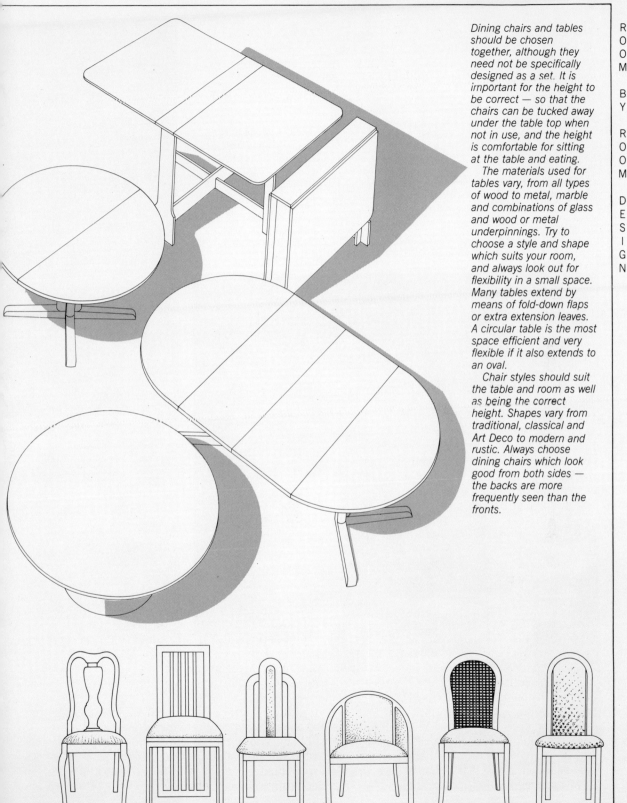

Dining chairs and tables should be chosen together, although they need not be specifically designed as a set. It is important for the height to be correct — so that the chairs can be tucked away under the table top when not in use, and the height is comfortable for sitting at the table and eating.

The materials used for tables vary, from all types of wood to metal, marble and combinations of glass and wood or metal underpinnings. Try to choose a style and shape which suits your room, and always look out for flexibility in a small space. Many tables extend by means of fold-down flaps or extra extension leaves. A circular table is the most space efficient and very flexible if it also extends to an oval.

Chair styles should suit the table and room as well as being the correct height. Shapes vary from traditional, classical and Art Deco to modern and rustic. Always choose dining chairs which look good from both sides — the backs are more frequently seen than the fronts.

These garden inspired living rooms (below and right) are both indoor/outdoor rooms incorporating the view as an integral part of the scheme and using plants to create a 'hot house' atmosphere.

In both rooms the furniture is elegant, almost opulent. Accessories are plentiful and carefully collected. The lighting draws attention to plants and objects of interest at night. The window treatments are both designed to let in maximum daylight, which can be controlled and screened,and to permit maximum exposure to the view.

An inspired display of treasured possessions at the dining end of a living room (above far right) is shown off against a coarse matting, with lamps acting as a colour contrast and providing illumination. An unusual collection of country style accessories (below far right) is enhanced with dried flowers, grasses and artichokes.

BEDROOMS

The bedroom is usually a highly personal room and this should be reflected in its particular style and decoration. Bedrooms come in all shapes and sizes from master bedrooms possibly with en suite dressing area or bathroom to single rooms used mainly for sleeping, dual-purpose rooms doubling up as spare room and study or rooms used by children, which may well also double up as playrooms.

A bedroom needs to accommodate clothes, sports and hobby equipment and personal items, as well as providing sleeping, relaxing and clothes-hanging facilities. Just like the kitchen, the bedroom storage space often has to be extensive and it is always wise to plan for much more storage than you think you need at the outset. If you are going to install any of the different types of fitted furniture, you will need to do your own measuring up and planning in advance, to ensure that you get exactly what you need.

The most important item of furniture in a bedroom, however, is not the storage but the bed. The choice is enormous – a dramatic four-poster, a romantic brass bedstead, a dual-purpose sofabed, a water bed, an air bed, a Futon , a simple divan or bunks for children's rooms. The bed should be chosen to reflect the image of the room. If you want a traditional room, for example, then look at bedsteads, four-posters, half-testers and Empire-style chaises longues and once you have made a decision, style the rest of the room round it.

The size of bed will depend on the space available and your requirements. Always buy a bed from a reputable store or bedding specialist and try it out before you buy. This means actually lying full length on several different beds, with your head supported on a pillow, until you are quite sure you have chosen the most comfortable and suitable bed. If you are buying a bed for somebody else, take them along to try it out, and in a shared situation, both partners should try the bed separately and together. You need not suffer if you are a completely different size from your partner, as many double beds are available as two separate mattresses with zips and link/press stud fittings – one sleeper can have a heavier gauge of spring than the other. Beds, apart from being comfortable for the sleeper as far as firmness is concerned, must be wide enough and long enough.

Beds come in certain recommended sizes (see right) but you can get special widths, lengths and

A large number of bed sizes are available as illustrated here (below and right). Taking the trouble to choose a bed that fits the occupants will ensure a good night's sleep. If there is a significant difference in weight and height between two partners, it may be worth investing in two half-size mattresses which can be zipped together. This facility is offered by the major bed manufacturers.

Measure the space available accurately before buying or moving a bed, allowing enough room for making the bed easily.

Standard sizes

| 190×190cm/ 6¼×3ft | 190×135cm/ 6¼×4½ft | 200×100cm/ 6½×3⅓ft | 200×150cm/ 6½×5ft |

Long an

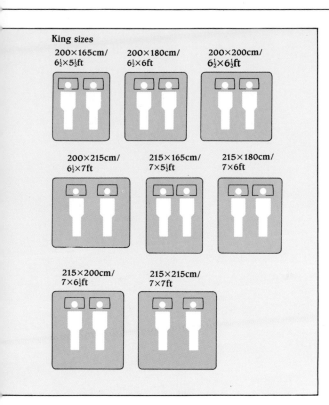

King sizes

200×165cm/ 6½×5½ft

200×180cm/ 6½×6ft

200×200cm/ 6½×6½ft

200×215cm/ 6½×7ft

215×165cm/ 7×5½ft

215×180cm/ 7×6ft

215×200cm/ 7×6½ft

215×215cm/ 7×7ft

BEDROOM SHAPES

Siting the bed or beds is the most important part of bedroom planning. Ideally they should not be under a window or in a draught. Try to organize a run of fitted cupboards along one wall.

A long, narrow bedroom (below far left) with windows on two sides has cupboards fitted to fill the narrow end wall, with dressing table incorporated. This helps foreshorten the room visually. Twin bedheads are placed to the door wall.

The small, square room (below centre) is given character with freestanding period furniture, which allows for seasonal changes. The winter position is shown. In summer the bedhead goes to the outside wall, with wardrobe and chest along the door wall. The L-shaped room adapted for two, (below right), has zoned areas for study, clothes storage and sleeping.

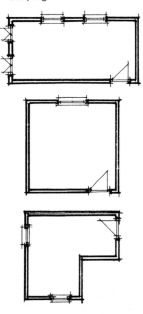

Square

L-shaped

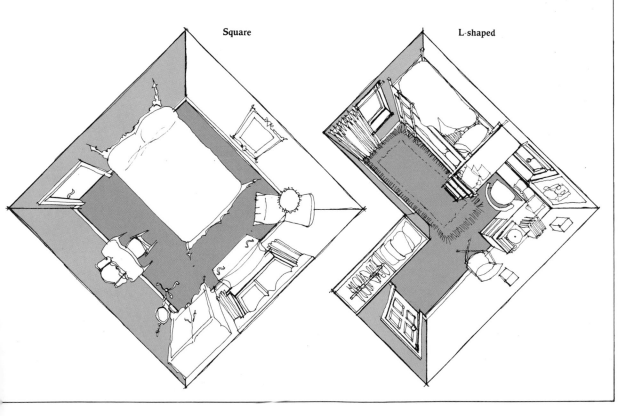

The traditional bedroom scheme (below) is based around a brass and wrought iron bedstead which also suits the architectural style of the room. Accessories have been selected with care to emphasize this look, and the decorative border/frieze and ceiling treatment make the tall ceiling appear lower.

The modern style bed sets the theme in this bedroom (left), *with its built-in headboard and bedside tables. The colour scheme, based on greys and yellows is warm but restful. The simple graphic pattern on the roller blinds, echoed in the draped bed canopy, softens the rather stark architectural style of the room. A place for everything in the bedside table/headboard* (far left) *includes concealed lighting to give a softly diffused glow, strong enough to permit bedtime reading.*

different shapes to order, including circular, oval, heart-shaped and King, Queen and Emperor sized beds.

Always buy a new base as well as a mattress if you are getting a sprung edge divan. The base of a bedstead may be firm enough to support a new mattress, but make sure if you buy a wooden bed with slatted base that you get the right type of mattress to go with it – some bed bases can be very firm and can put a strain on the mattress. Never put an old mattress on a new base, and vice versa. It is also important to check on the condition of a bed and mattress after a few years' use. They should be changed fairly regularly, after about twenty years for top quality beds and after about ten for lesser quality. Always test any spare beds occasionally before you subject guests to an uncomfortable night! If you are planning a dual-purpose room, the sofa bed or studio bed should be comfortable for both purposes. Some of the simple sofa beds, which are made from foam slabs, open to make a comfortable occasional overnight bed, but these are not suitable for use every night. If you need a

convertible, which is to be used nightly for sleeping and daily for sitting, look for a sofa bed which has a separate mattress and wire or sprung base hidden inside. A divan bed, with tailored cover or throw-over covering can be more suitable for day and night use, but it does need a very firm sprung edge. This type of bed should be tested and changed more frequently than single use beds. There are other beds suitable for use in a dual-purpose situation, which fold up into a cupboard, or even convert into a coffee table or other item of furniture. Again, these are good for occasional use, except for the fold-up (Murphy) bed which can be used nightly.

Planning bedrooms

As most bedrooms have to be planned for storage, sleeping and other activities, again your plan should be worked out accurately on scaled paper. With a child's room, you will need to allow for growing up and changing needs (see page 79). With rooms for other people, try to think ahead, and plan for future as well as present needs.

Classical divan bed — sprung base and spring interior mattress (1). Classical bedstead with foot and head ends, joined by rails with a firm base (open mesh wire sprung or slatted wood) and separate mattress (2). A four poster (3) can be modern or traditional, depending on the type of posts and fabric drapes. The canopy may be part of the frame and posts or can be created using a pelmet or valance with fabric. Posts can also be simulated with draped fabric. A single Futon (4) forms an oversize chair by day and unfurls at night to become a single bed. The stylish modern bed (5) is a development of the classical bedstead, which can be made in metal, wood or plastic.

In many rooms there is a natural place to site storage. There might be two recesses to each side of a fireplace which could be used for fitted cupboards or a cupboard could be built one side with fitted shelves on the other. If the recesses are not very deep, the cupboards can be built to project slightly, and be joined by shelves or a dressing table across the breast. If you do not want anything too permanent, fix adjustable shelves and hanging rails in the recesses, and fit pull-down roller blinds, Roman blinds or curtains with a pelmet.

A long wall may be a natural place to put a whole run of cupboards and this might incorporate a shower in its own cabinet or a basin/vanity unit, which can be concealed, or be part of the storage wall. In some rooms, the wall featuring the door is the only unbroken area and it is possible to build along such a wall, concealing the door behind cupboard doors for a completely streamlined effect. In other rooms it is better to build along one wall, leaving an alcove in the centre for the bedhead. The wardrobes can be linked with top cupboards or shelves which go across the gap, giving space for concealed lighting below. Alternatively, use the space for a wall hanging or picture.

Again, if you do not want permanent storage, hanging space can be provided by a portable dress

If a bedroom has a chimney breast, the recesses on either side are the ideal place to site 'clothes and clobber' storage (1). For temporary storage, fit adjustable shelves and dress rails and hang curtains instead of doors (2). Fit high level storage cupboards with open shelves beneath for books, television and other objects (3). Make a feature of the wall with ceiling-mounted spotlights (4). Fit permanent wardrobe storage with louvred doors (5). Use half for a dressing area and half for clothes (6).

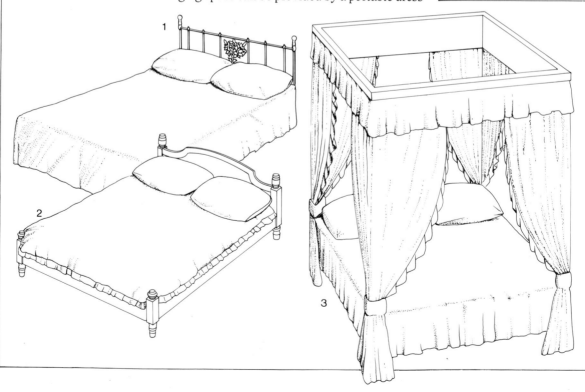

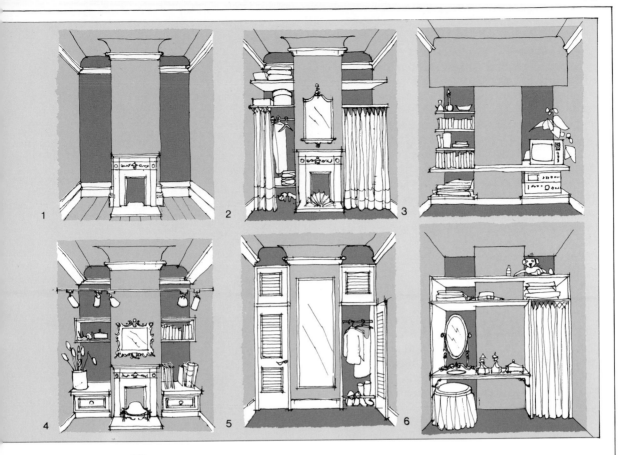

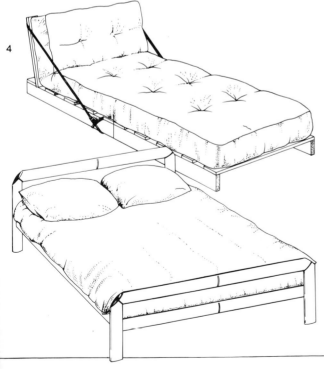

rail and other storage by stackable wire racks or adjustable shelves, which can be hidden behind curtains, vertical louvre blinds or fabric panels or temporarily boxed in. In some rooms, a series of folding doors or portable screens make a better method of concealment.

If the room is large, it may be possible to build wardrobes and other storage out from the wall, at right angles to it, dividing the room into a sleeping and a dressing area. The bedhead can be placed to the back of the run of cupboards, and the cupboards can be decorated to match the room, or clad with wood, cork or fabric. If you do not want to form such a permanent division, but like the idea of zoning the areas, a curtain, lace or fabric panel or vertical blinds can be used to separate sleeping and dressing areas. In a shared situation, where possibly two or more children are using the room, it is often better to give them separate halves, and make each of them responsible for their own part. Dividing with wardrobes, chests and other storage furniture can work well here, and blinds can be used to close any gaps.

If the room is for two adults, a flexible approach to storage and planning is even more important, and may not necessarily mean dividing everything up. The main master bedroom, for example, is usually the largest. It works well to have an en suite bathroom with this type of bedroom, and it is sometimes possible to convert an adjoining room or part of the landing to provide this. If you want to convert and extend, try to include such an arrangement in your initial plans.

Try to plan for somewhere to sit and relax in a large bedroom. A comfortable corner, with chairs, small table and light for reading or sewing, for example, possibly complete with tea or coffee making equipment. If space will not allow, it is sometimes possible to position a small settee or chaise longue parallel with the bottom of a double bed. A mini office can also be useful in a large master bedroom. A desk might be included as an attractive piece of furniture, which can also be used for clothes as well as stationery storage. If the main bedroom is also to be used for relaxing, a television set might be included in the furnishings. If it is to be watched from bed it may be possible to site it inside a top wall-mounted cupboard or on top of another item of furniture.

Although the master bedroom is usually the main one, the biggest bedroom may well be given to children as a bedroom/playroom, or be used as a flatlet – to accommodate a teenage or older child (see page 79). Alternatively, it may be given to an elderly relative as a 'granny flat' or if you work from home, it may have to become the office or studio, and double up as guest or main bedroom. Always think about a room's function and plan carefully to make maximum use of its size and shape.

If your bedrooms are tall, you can also plan widthwise. It may be practical to incorporate a sleeping platform on top of built-in furniture or on top of a raised plinth. You could also install a shower, a wardrobe or other facilities under a built-up bed. Before doing this you may have to make elevated room plans (see page 13) to help work out the proportions.

Do not discount the space over the bed in lower rooms – it is sometimes possible to mount storage units on the ceiling above the bed. They will need to be firmly screwed into the ceiling and can be used for 'dead' storage. You could also conceal lighting and suspend curtains or drapes from the units to simulate a four-poster bed. You could run a shelf

Shared bedrooms may have to be divided to provide a separate space for each person or a large bedroom can be zoned into sleeping and dressing areas. The wardrobe cupboards are placed at right-angles to the long wall (above), *with flap-down desk top and doors opening on one side, mirror and shelves recessed on the other, making a cosy corner for each single bed.*

Vertical venetian blinds fit into a sloping window recess (above right). *The sloping ceiling is coloured to match the blinds and the wall of built-in wardrobes.*

The large bedroom (left) with important fabric drapes to suggest a four-poster bed, also provides a quiet corner for reading, sewing or conversation away from the hassle of family life. Try to provide a place to sit even in smaller rooms, such as a small easy chair or a padded ottoman at the foot of the bed.

right round the bedroom above the level of the curtain rail, excluding the wardrobe wall. You could also run a hanging rail under the shelf to provide additional temporary space for clothes and bags. Match the colour of the shelf and rail with other items of furniture.

To plan practically, work out exactly what you need on scaled paper in the usual way, remembering to allow for opening doors and drawers, moving round the furniture and pulling out the bed for making. Remember that bunk beds can be very heavy to move. If you are going to call in a firm of experts to design and make the furniture, they will probably make scale drawings themselves, but it pays to have done your initial preparation work so that you can brief them properly.

The look

Bedrooms can be decorated in many different styles to create the required atmosphere. Again, the main emphasis should be provided by colour and pattern, but the furniture you select will also dictate the chosen look to some extent. Any built-in or storage furniture should be in keeping with the overall decorating theme, or should be treated so that it blends in with the scheme. If the storage units are attractive in themselves, they can become the focal point.

Colour will help create the right atmosphere, and can be chosen to relax or stimulate, make a room more intimate or cosy or create a room that is spacious and elegant. In most bedrooms, accessories are again important, and can help a great deal towards achieving the finished look. Bed linen in particular can coordinate or contrast with the scheme and should be chosen carefully as an integral part of the room's furnishings. A bedcover can transform a room during the day. If the bedding is designed to be seen, choose several different designs and colours for variety. Cool pastel colours can look refreshing and light in summer, and strong, warmer ones will seem cosy in winter.

Surfaces in the bedroom usually tend to be softer, more luxurious than elsewhere, but it does depend on whose room it is. An adult bedroom may be decorated in pale colours and have long-pile carpets because it will be treated carefully, whereas a child's room or teenage bedsitting room will need tough, washable surfaces and practical colours.

LIGHTING FOR DRESSING TABLES

Dressing table and bathroom vanitory unit lighting needs to be strong and clear for making up. The light should shine on to the face, but not into the eyes. Theatrical-style bulbs surrounding a mirror, or running down either side will provide a good light for shaving and making up (1, 2). Fluorescent strips down each side or across the top and bottom of the mirror will also light the face clearly (3) — for a softer glow, use several tubes of narrow strip lighting, filtered through a louvred baffle.

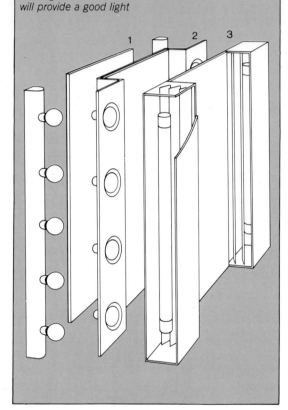

Lighting Light the dressing table, make-up area, vanity unit or dressing area with direct lighting, independently switched. Light the bed area with well-shaded direct bedside or wall-mounted lamps, one for each side of the bed in a shared bedroom. Check the height for the light fittings by sitting in a comfortable reading position and angling the light to shine on the open page of the book. Light the room with subdued background lighting on a dimmer switch, controlled from both the door and the bed. Light the insides of any deep storage units or wardrobes, with the switch fitted to the door jamb. In a dual-purpose bedroom, include direct lighting for a study or hobby area.

SAFETY HINTS FOR CHILDREN'S ROOMS

Children's rooms should be practical and pretty, but above all safe. At each stage of development there are new hazards.

• Never heat a child's room with an electric bar or gas fire. Central heating radiators are best, or oil-filled thermo-statically controlled electric radiators. Or use an adequately guarded wall-mounted infra-red heater, positioned out of reach.

• Check all windows for safety — sash windows and louvred vents are usually safe, but most other types, particularly casement and pivoting windows, can be a hazard. If necessary fit bars.

• Keep light fittings out of reach and install electric sockets with safety shutters so the child cannot poke anything into the holes. Site light switches where the child can reach them easily.

• Remove any inside bolts or keys from a child's door (do this in the bathroom and lavatory while a child is at an age likely to lock him/herself in).

• Make sure furniture is safe and there is no possibility of pulling over

tall cupboards or stacked items. Use brackets or wall-mounting to prevent this happening. If the furniture is painted, make sure the paint is non-toxic and safe — special nursery paints are available for walls and furniture.

• Make sure cots and play pens conform to

government requirements — this means safe sides and ends with bars spaced so that the child cannot push his/her head through.

• The floor should be a safe play area — fit smooth, washable flooring, and avoid slippery rugs or those which turn up at the corners.

Rooms to grow up in

Planning, decorating and furnishing rooms for children can be a problem. The different stages of a child's life usually mean different furnishing and decorative needs, and it is important to plan a room which allows for expansion as the child develops.

Do not immediately rush out to fill the room with furniture. Think carefully about the plan before you start. A built-in cupboard can be designed in such a way that it will last through nursery to bedsit – adjustable shelves and hanging space should make this possible. Start off with some basic items of free-standing furniture and select these from a range which can be added to later on, checking that there will be continuity of supply when you order. You may find the most practical way of planning is to start out with the final stage and work backwards.

Infancy The needs of a baby are relatively simple, and the nursery should be more of a pleasant and practical room for the parents. The baby needs somewhere to sleep (crib or carry cot), you need somewhere to store essentials plus a convenient flat surface for a nappy change and a place for a bath and nappy bucket. The parents will need somewhere to sit when feeding the infant, and it is worth considering installing an intercom system, linked to the downstairs rooms, so that you can hear when the baby cries.

Apart from the specific items of nursery equipment, a proper changing area which later becomes a desk/play top and dressing table is a practical piece of furniture, which can be made from two chests of drawers, linked by a continuous top. Decorate everything very simply at this stage, and avoid too many cuddly toy motifs. Keep the furniture plain and add patterns in wall coverings, curtains or attractive nursery borders which can easily be changed when needed. A washable flooring (softened by washable rugs) is the best treatment underfoot.

The toddler This is the stage when the child becomes mobile and wants play space. At this stage, a drop-sided cot (there are types which transform and extend to make a bed), a toy box, high-chair and play pen may all become necessary. It is sensible at this time to remove the chair for the parents, and perhaps any trolley used for baby equipment. The decorations may well be altered at this stage, and a roller blind which obliterates the

Children's rooms with a sense of style. A basically neutral and simply furnished scheme for a teenager (right) relies on posters and postcard/picture montage to add individuality. This treatment can be a continually changing scene as different hobbies, interests and lifestyles develop. An *eye-catching mural* (below) fills one wall and creeps round the corner along the window wall. This treatment transforms a square box-like room and can be adapted, or added to, when tastes or colour schemes change.

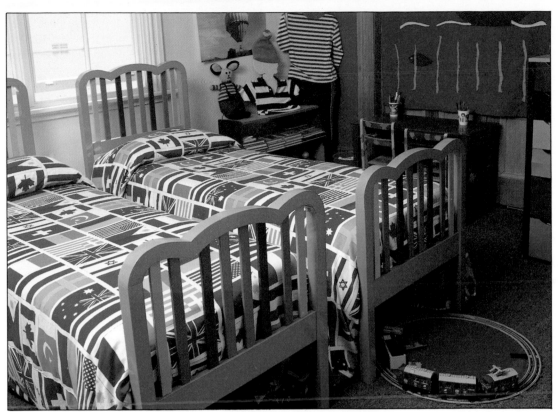

The bright, primary colour scheme (above), designed to stimulate the imaginations of younger children, is carried through from the painted bedsteads on to patterned bedcovers and into the accessories and wall treatment. Bright fold-down chairs (left) have been given a highly personalized decorative treatment, which coordinates with the rest of the painted furniture in the bedroom. They are particularly practical as they can be folded up and hung on large colourful hooks on the wall, or stacked in a cupboard, when extra floor space is needed for train layouts or games.

light can be added to the window to help persuade the toddler to sleep on warm summer evenings. This and the next stage of childhood are still fairly messy, so store the rugs.

The kindergarten child usually wants a dual-purpose room, one which doubles as bedroom/playroom. It needs to include a play area, a space to make a mess with paints and plasticine, a blackboard/scribble board and a normal bed. Bunk beds can be sensible if the room is likely to have to be shared with another child. The decorations may change slightly to involve the favourite television character of the moment. A change of curtains or fresh wallpaper will probably be sufficient to create the desired effect.

The school child may well have quite strong ideas about how the room should look. By this time, hobbies and interests have developed, which may mean storage for bulky sports equipment. A desk and bookshelves and improved clothes' storage may be required and the decorative scheme may have to be changed again. At this stage the flooring could be changed, depending on the room and the child's activities. Practical possibilities include carpet tiles, cork and seagrass matting.

The pre-teen child wants a room where friends can come to chat, work, read and play. Technology is likely to influence this age group, and computers may well be the most important thing, so they need a large desk and lots of power sockets. Hobbies can be important too and they may well want a railway layout on a pulley to be lowered at will, or possibly a table tennis table if there is space.

At this age too, definite ideas on decoration, furniture and design may begin to emerge. These should be encouraged and the child persuaded to help make items, perhaps even to try their hand at some supervised decorating. Lots of storage space will also be essential.

The teenager usually likes a total change of scene. They may ask for a new sofabed which can also be used to entertain friends. Remember though, it will be slept on every night, so it must be firm and suitable for both sitting and sleeping. An Oriental Futon might be suitable, otherwise you may be able to compromise with tailored covers and cushions on a low divan bed. Floor cushions are a good idea for seating. The decorations may change

drastically – the room might be painted black with a star-studded ceiling, for example, or disco lighting may be wired in against a mainly primary-coloured scheme.

The young adult, between leaving school and attending college or starting a job, may not be around for long. They may want their room to be their own place, with increased facilities, such as a shower cubicle, making a separate washing/dressing area, or a kitchenette. Be realistic about how long they are likely to stay or how often they will come back before investing in major alterations. In a large, older-style property, where the ceilings are high, it may be possible to use split-level planning, and build a sleeping platform, with shower, kitchen or desk facilities below.

Infancy
The room is really a nursery at this stage, requiring comfortable changing facilities and washable floor surfaces, softened by rugs.

The toddler
A safe room where the child can make a mess. The crib is exchanged for a cot, the nursing chair goes and is replaced by a play pen, the bath gives way to a high chair.

Infancy

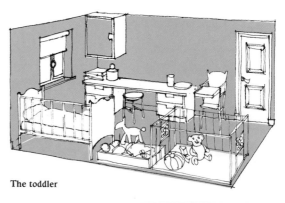

The toddler

The looks

This will be a changing theme throughout a child's development years. Small children like bright colours, so starting with a pastel nursery image and then adding colour in accents is one approach. Brighter colours and treatments could be added as the room becomes a playroom/bedroom, and latterly, as the room becomes a complete living area for the fashionable teenager, a coordinated wall covering and accessory image can be developed.

Style will depend on the child's age and interests. With children's rooms the question of specific styling does not arise in quite the same way as for other rooms in the house. The particular tastes of the room's owner will dictate style.

Surfaces above all need to be practical, particularly during infancy and early childhood. Washable flooring, wipe-down surfaces on furniture, washable woodwork and walls papered with vinyl-coated wallpaper are the most practical surfaces for the first four stages.

Because of the need for constant change and updating of the scheme, to keep up with the child's requirements, it is sometimes wise to have the main surfaces as plain as possible, and to introduce different designs in wallpaper friezes and borders on plain-painted walls. Alternatively, a wall covering with a striking design can be introduced on perhaps one wall only, or in the curtains, roller blinds, bed linens and other accessories which can be easily changed when they are outgrown.

The kindergarten child
Plenty of play space is now needed. The first bed replaced the cot and the changing area becomes a play/desk/painting surface. A blackboard is sited on one wall.

The school child
The desk/changing area is adapted again and a cupboard is added to provide more storage. A large toy box doubles as sitting and play space with instant tidy-up-facility!

The pre-teen child
A drop-down table top is sited next to the desk, which has TV and computer facilities. A coffee table is added and the bed gets a tailored cover.

The teenager
Storage for clothes and hobbies now becomes a priority. The storage system is streamlined and the room takes on the air of a sophisticated bedsitting room.

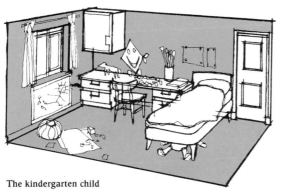

The kindergarten child

The pre-teen child

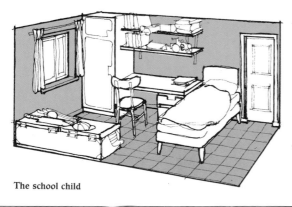

The school child

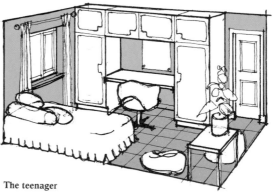

The teenager

Many rooms have to be dual or multi-purpose — and the design has to overcome a space problem.

In a tall room, split-level living is possible (right). The bed is mounted on a long-legged platform with ladder access, leaving the area underneath free for desk/hobbies/dressing table. In some multi-function rooms, cooking or washing (shower and basin) facilities can be built under a raised platform bed. This long, large bedroom (far right) doubles as a second bathroom, with a radiator used a divider. The bathroom area can be curtained off, if necessary, by floor-to-ceiling curtains mounted on a track embedded in the ceiling.

DUAL-PURPOSE ROOMS

In many houses and flats, the shortage of space means a spare bedroom is an unlikely luxury. Any extra room has to be multi-functional, not just dual-purpose, and some large rooms become complete living areas. If a room is to double up as a study or office and bedroom, and it is only to be used occasionally for overnight guests, it should be planned primarily for the main function. This is where multi-purpose furniture is ideal, but it is essential to remember when choosing sofabeds or studio beds that if they are only going to be slept on rarely, they should be comfortable to sit on. If they are to be slept on every night, then they must be firm and comfortable as both bed and sofa. A futon is a practical solution here. Wooden bases for futons come in a variety of styles and colour stains, and can easily be blended in with the overall colour schemes.

In some cases the sitting room or main living area may be the only place to put up an overnight guest. Again convertible furniture should be selected primarily for sitting comfort. A separate dining room can also be used as a study, sewing and hobbies room and second sitting room as well as a possible spare bedroom. In the bedroom/playroom, bunk beds, platform beds or coloured scaffolding can become part of the play area. Some fantasy furniture has recently been developed for children – beds and bunks like space ships, buses, Cinderella's coach and Wendy houses which convert into chests of drawers and dressing tables. Before selecting anything like this, consider the practicalities and lifespan and read the section on planning rooms for children (see page 79).

In larger properties, a room may well be used for many different purposes, such as a games and billiards room and conservatory, an office or studio, a music room, a gym or workout room, or a dressmaking or other craft area.

This range of multi-functional steel-framed furniture based on the scaffolding principle can be constructed to form bed platform, ladder and desk (left). Alternatively it can be reconstructed to form a climbing frame. Later it might form part of a teenage High tech bedroom, and eventually become a tower platform for decorating.

D
E
S
I
G
N

I
N

P
R
A
C
T
I
C
E

Planning multi-purpose rooms

The starting point will be the same as with any other room, but sorting it all out may be harder, because of the need to combine storage and facilities with comfort, function and good looks. It will definitely mean making scale plans to see how everything fits in. Again look at the basic shape and size of the room and decide exactly what you want to accommodate in the way of furniture and storage as well as planning for the various activities for which the room is likely to be used. Decide on the main function of the room and give this top priority, fitting the other requirements round it.

For example, if you have to work at home and need an office, but it doubles as a spare bedroom, try to provide a storage unit, which will include space for hanging guests' clothes, select a desk or units which will double as a dressing-table, and combine storage for files with drawers suitable for clothes. Select a sofabed or chairs which convert to single beds, and which can make a comfortable discussion area. Group them round a coffee table, which becomes a bedside table, allowing enough space for the sofa or chairs to open out for sleeping.

In some cases, a fold-down bed which disappears into the wall, as part of a run of storage cupboards, may be a more practical solution.

Folding or trestle-type tables can also be useful in the dining room or living room, if the space is cramped. In an office or study, the table can be a work surface, desk or drawing board, but fold away neatly when not needed.

In some cases, when a multi-functional room is also used for recreation, then the furniture and surface treatments will centre around that particular hobby. Some can be messy, like painting, pottery, woodwork and metalwork, and will need adequate equipment like an easel, kiln, work bench or lathe. If this is the case, the equipment will take up some room and may be heavy. You will also need to bring in heavy raw materials, so try to site the room on a ground floor. Sometimes building an extension, or converting part of the garage is the most practical answer.

Some hobbies may need fireproof materials, and others could involve installing adequate sound proofing, to protect neighbours and the rest of the family. All this should be thought about very carefully at the beginning of your scheme, and if

In a design/craft studio which also has to be used for sleeping, a hammock is slung between two stout beams (right) — *it can be taken down and rolled up if extra space is required. Hammocks can be used in children's rooms, but be prepared for tips and spills if the average age is below 15!*

A clever multi-storage system can be used to fill an entire wall or recess, in any room in the house. The modular system includes open shelves, boxes, trays, drawers, glass or close-fronted doors and connecting blocks, so it can be built to the required height. The 'Book' Shelving System shown here (far right) *is adapted to make a desk/dining table and storage in a dual-purpose dining room/study.*

necessary, professional advice should be sought. If you plan to convert your attic or loft for one of these work rooms, think about possible fire risk, noise and whether the joists need strengthening. It may make more sense to put a bedroom/bathroom complex into the roof space, or possibly a sitting room, and to convert a room downstairs into the recreation room.

If a room is to be used as a music room, and perhaps to double as a spare bedroom or dining room/study, it may have to accommodate a piano. Uprights are not too difficult to hide behind screens, blinds or curtains if you do not want them to be an integral part of the furnishing scheme, but because of its size, a grand or baby grand piano is difficult to disguise. Try making it a focal point instead. A large exotic shawl or a patchwork quilt in flamboyant 1920s style thrown over it will both cover and protect it. Upright pianos can be decorated in any of the painted techniques to give them a newer look.

If a music room needs a large collection of sound equipment and sophisticated electronics, make sure these are housed in a safe place and can be locked away from curious small fingers.

Soundproofing will be essential in such a room. If a room is to accommodate a major game such as table tennis, the table will take up a lot of space, so think about the types that can be folded away or others which can be raised to the roof by means of a pulley. In a smaller room, which has to double as a bedroom, stacking beds under the table during the day might be a practical way of coping. A hammock can easily be used, especially if a room is decorated to match in nautical or tropical style. In a taller room, a bed built on to a platform will leave space underneath to accommodate a grand piano, games table, mini office or other essential furniture. (For bedrooms which double as bedsitting rooms or bedroom/dressing rooms, see pages 70 to 83.)

Note that any of these dual or multi-purpose rooms will need specialized lighting and possibly extra power sockets. Snooker or billiards tables, for example, usually have overhead screened lighting and desks and drawing boards will need direct lighting, possibly with angled lamps. Think about all these aspects in relation to your overall furnishing and storage plan.

Multi-functional rooms come in many shapes, sizes and styles. The three pictures on this page (above, above right and right) are aspects of one long, large study and bathroom area. The ceiling in the bathroom area is slightly lower and is used for recessed downlighters, and a large air-extraction unit — essential with bath and books in such close proximity!

The colour scheme is carried through the two sections of the room, based on subtle blue-grey walls and a slate-tiled floor — this treatment is taken up on to the bath panel. Warm touches are added in the rose-pink upholstered reading chair and the brilliant coral and turquoise festoon drapes — coral, red and pink are also added in bathroom accessories.

Accessories include

steam-loving plants, but pictures are mainly framed photographs.

This large open plan studio (above) *is used for sitting, entertaining, dining, sleeping and painting. The gallery above provides sleeping and clothes storage accommodation, with bathroom leading off, and is reached via the wrought-iron spiral staircase.*

The colour scheme is neutral and relies on changing accessories and paintings to provide the necessary colour accents and alterations in mood. Such all-in-one areas are usually custom-built, or part of converted older properties like barns, chapels, school houses,disused railway buidings, etc.

An office in the kitchen (right). *In many homes, the kitchen is the centre of family activity so it may well be the best place to do the accounts, catch up with correspondence, keep personal records and house a telephone. In this house the desk doubles as a table for informal meals. Again good extraction of steam (and cooking smells) is essential if papers are to be safe from condensation — a built-in hood and extractor fan are sited over the cooking hob.*

If you have a large kitchen, it may make sense to plan it to double up as kitchen/family living area or playroom — so long as the safety aspect is considered carefully.

Planning for one-room living

This type of room is definitely multi-purpose and has to be planned as such. In some houses the whole downstairs area might be open plan and so is virtually one-room living, even if there is a place to sleep upstairs. In other situations, where one big room is being used, the sleeping accommodation may well be provided on a gallery or platform. But the important thing to remember, when planning rooms for living, eating, sleeping, entertaining and perhaps cooking and working in as well, is to consider the requirements of the person who will use the room most and to work out the most streamlined design to accommodate all the necessary features.

If you are making a room into a bedsitting room, you will need to consider any hobbies and interests, and whether the room will be used for entertaining friends. The room may well be used for studying or working or might need to accommodate more than one person. If on the other hand the room is to house an elderly relative, who may possibly be partially disabled, ease of access will be of prime importance. Being close to a bathroom, lavatory or shower is also extremely important. If the room is for staff, to give them privacy while living in, then the requirements will be different again. Consider installing a separate entrance from outside, although this may involve fairly major structural work.

Again, splitting a tall room by raising the bed on a platform and installing storage, desk, bathroom or cooking facilities underneath is a good way of getting in all the necessary items, but remember to make adequate arrangements for ventilation. In a lower room you could build a platform to accommodate the mattress or bed. Alternatively, you can use it for the dining table or desk and then use the space underneath for storage. In a study or work environment, low filing cabinets and storage drawers can be used to form the base of the platform. Look at the range of office and industrial furniture now available. It is often more practical, stronger and less expensive than domestic furniture. The room can then be decorated in a bright, High tech style. The space above the bed is often under-utilized, and sometimes the bed can be positioned parallel to the wall between two storage wardrobes, with top cupboards above and drawers below, to create a 'bed-in-a-cupboard'. The space between the bed and upper cupboard, should allow for getting in and out with ease. Curtains or blinds can close it off during the daytime. A real bed which folds up into a cupboard (a Murphy bed) as part of a run of storage can also be used in the one-room-living situation, with a convertible sofabed also providing extra sleeping accommodation for guests, when necessary. Alternatively, a mattress can be placed on top of some linked cube storage units.

Quite often, a divan bed can double as a sofa in dual-purpose and one-room living areas, placing it parallel to the wall and using a tailored cover, with a collection of cushions along the back and bolster cushions each side to form 'arms'. A wall-mounted pole with back cushions suspended from it can also be used to create a similar effect or a bed can be covered Oriental-style with a colourful rug and piled high with exotic-looking cushions. Again, make sure a bed used in this way is of good quality, and firm-edged enough for sitting and sleeping.

The sitting area in such a room should be treated as the sitting area in a living room – sometimes a conversation 'pit' can be an effective way of making more of one room, and it will probably be more practical to plan a dining area with fold-away or dual-purpose furniture.

Again, when planning such a room on paper, always an essential exercise, remember to allow for space for people actually to walk around the furniture – and to use it, open drawers, doors, or pull back chairs from tables or desks.

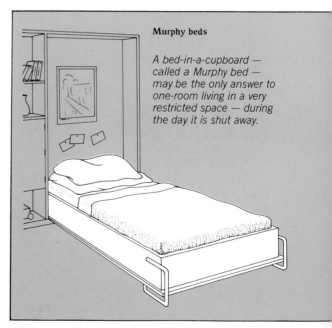

Murphy beds

A bed-in-a-cupboard — called a Murphy bed — may be the only answer to one-room living in a very restricted space — during the day it is shut away.

Sofabeds

Sofa or studio beds come in many shapes, sizes and styles — some simply unfold to form a base and mattress (single or double), while others have a folding base spring and mattress hidden inside the seat of the sofa, which is easily pulled out to form a double bed.

Futons

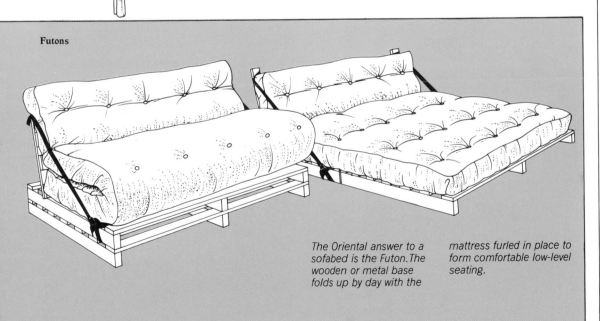

The Oriental answer to a sofabed is the Futon. The wooden or metal base folds up by day with the mattress furled in place to form comfortable low-level seating.

One-room living only works well if the room is adequately planned and properly furnished for all functions. This living/eating/dining/sleeping area (left) relies on flexible furniture for its success — the director-style chairs fold up when extra space is needed, the sofa becomes a bed and the desk/serving table behind it can be taken down.

The split-level studio (right) has desk and office space under the highly placed bed, with a dual purpose dining table in the centre, and the sitting area (not seen) can accommodate extra overnight guests.

Another flexibly furnished room (below) has folding chrome-framed chairs which can be hung up on the wall out of the way.

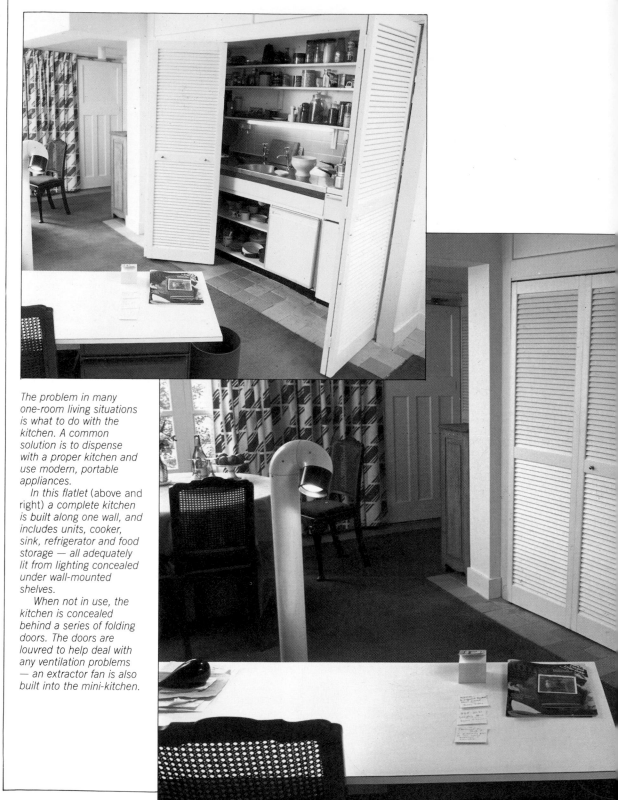

The problem in many one-room living situations is what to do with the kitchen. A common solution is to dispense with a proper kitchen and use modern, portable appliances.

In this flatlet (above and right) a complete kitchen is built along one wall, and includes units, cooker, sink, refrigerator and food storage — all adequately lit from lighting concealed under wall-mounted shelves.

When not in use, the kitchen is concealed behind a series of folding doors. The doors are louvred to help deal with any ventilation problems — an extractor fan is also built into the mini-kitchen.

The look

The main problem with multi-purpose and one-room living areas is lack of space both in reality and visually, so keep the shapes in larger areas simple and streamlined to preserve a feeling of space. Any unnecessary clutter will only serve to minimize the available space. Mirrors can help to magnify the apparent size of a very small room (see page 152) so use them cleverly perhaps to front a run of cupboards along one wall, or as a panel in the darkest area to reflect light as well. Panelling the back of the door with mirrors is another alternative. Even if the room is not very large, try at least to zone the areas visually, but avoid heavy dividers. You can do this by a change of floor covering, or by a change of levels (previously mentioned) or by the way you arrange the furniture.

Style The important thing is always to follow basic styling principles with this type of room, as there is so much furniture to include it can easily become a design disaster.

Colour In this type of room where space is limited, a simple, neutral scheme works well with colour accents provided by accessories. Monochromatic schemes based on different values of one colour also come into their own. Do not change the colour scheme or decorations too abruptly from area to area, but use coordinated ranges cleverly to give one large living and sleeping area two distinct personalities. But colour and pattern will need to be chosen to suit the purpose of the room too – brighter and more stimulating ones for children's, young people's and games rooms and more restrained ones for rooms which are used for sleeping and relaxing. Colour accents, added in the form of accessories, can also be doubled up. One set can be used for the main purpose of the room, when it is an office, for example, and changed for another set when it takes on its second function, such as entertaining.

Surfaces will probably get harder wear than in other rooms, so they need to be tough and practical. The flooring in a games room, or where a hobby is really messy, should be similar to the one you would put into the kitchen – quarry tiles, cork tiles, linoleum, cushion flooring, studded rubber flooring – but it can be softened with rugs. Upholstery will take rougher treatment too, and two sets of tailored or loose covers may be more practical than fixed fabric. Furniture surfaces and walls should be washable.

Lighting in a dual-purpose room will be determined by the different functions. Make sure any desk area is adequately lit. You might need a light for typing or controlling a computer or other keyboard which should come from behind and above. You should also have subdued background lighting, adequate direct lighting for reading and any other tasks. Make sure storage, files or bookshelves are functionally lit, and separately controlled.

Tricks of the Light

All too often, the way a room is lit is only considered at the final stage of decoration, when the accessories are added. Light fittings and lamps are often considered as accessories and lamps particularly can be finishing touches, but the light source, its position and all wiring and cabling, should all be decided upon at the planning stage.

Lighting can be used in many ways – to emphasize and enhance or even distort a feature, to dramatize or minimize the mode of decoration or apparently to alter the shape of a room. Like colour and pattern, lighting is an interior design tool which can be used to create atmosphere and style with maximum effect.

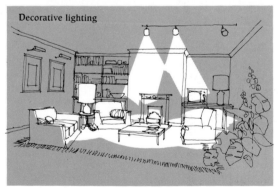

The sitting room (below) *is lit flexibly to provide good illumination for all functions with separate controls. Background lighting is provided by pools of light thrown up and down from table* lamps. *Direct or task lighting comes from spots, strategically placed on ceiling-mounted track. Decorative lighting floods pictures from special picture lights, individually mounted.*

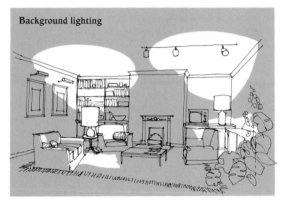

halls, stairs and landing areas and adds an extra dimension in kitchens and bathrooms. The level of background lighting can be further controlled with dimmer switches.

Direct or task lighting provides adequate illumination for the various jobs about the home. Good direct lighting is essential in the kitchen for lighting up food preparation surfaces, the cooker, the sink and laundry area; in the bathroom for shaving and doing make-up; in the bedroom for dressing tables and reading in bed; in bedsitting rooms for working at a desk or a hobby area; in the living area for highlighting the dining table, reading or coping with any specific work area; in the nursery, for changing the baby; in the hall, stair or landing area for illuminating stair treads and risers and telephone or cloakroom areas.

Decorative or accent lighting is used to 'shape' the room or draw attention to a particular area or feature in a room. It may be used to emphasize a collection of beautiful objects, to illuminate a painting or a group of paintings or to spotlight a selection of houseplants or a piece of statuary.

BASIC TYPES OF LIGHTING
There are three basic types of lighting and most rooms will have two, if not all three, types.

Background lighting provides a soft level of light throughout an area, particularly important in living areas and bedrooms. It is often desirable in

TYPES OF LIGHTING

Once you have decided on the type of lighting you require and roughly where it will be sited, light fittings have to be selected. Function as well as style has to be considered. Lighting stores and departments display a bewildering selection, but are a good place to choose basic items.

If you need advice, either call in an expert lighting designer or go to a lighting specialist supplier.

Spotlights and tracks

Freestanding lamps

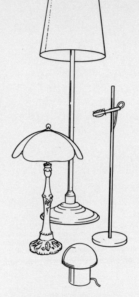

Hanging lights

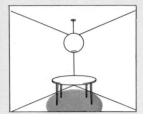

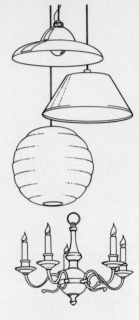

Desk lamps

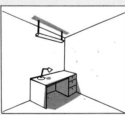

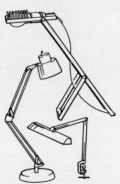

Desk lamps can be freestanding or clip-on. They provide concentrated areas of light and should be adjustable so that the fall of light can be altered.

Spotlights can either be mounted directly on to ceilings or walls or in track systems. They can be used as accent lighting to highlight objects or pictures, or as angled light in a work area, for example directed at the cooker, sink and food preparation areas in the kitchen. A spot may be designed to hold an ordinary bulb, a special spot bulb with an internal silvered reflector for intensity, or the spot itself may house a low voltage transformer which will cast a narrow beam of light on to a specific item.

Tracks offer a flexible approach to lighting. They can be fixed across the ceiling or down the wall. Light beams can be crossed at steep angles so that people in the room do not look directly into the beam of light.

A number of freestanding lamps fitted with dimmer switches around the room provide very flexible background light. Lamp shades can be selected to cast the required amount of light and to control its intensity, as well as being decorative accessories in their own right. Directional light for reading can be provided by adjustable table lamps.

A pendant or hanging light sited in the centre of the ceiling is the most common form of ceiling light. The height at which the shade is hung and the type of shade will affect the intensity of the light. A larger shade will tend to cast a softer and more subtle light.

Pendant lights provide good general light, but they tend to flatten shadows and divide a room, throwing light halfway down the walls.

They are very useful over a dining table, particularly if a rise-and-fall fixture is used.

Uplighters   **Downlighters**

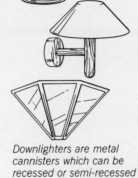

Uplighters can be used to create very interesting shadow effects in a room. They can be positioned behind plants, beneath glass shelves or in corners. They can also be directed to highlight objects or pictures dramatically.

Downlighters are metal cannisters which can be recessed or semi-recessed into ceilings to cast pools of light. A spot bulb can be used to provide a concentrated circle of light or a floodlight to cast a wider pool of light.

Downlighters can make colour more brilliant and moulding more effective, but they need to be carefully positioned. Use sparingly in the sitting room, where table lamps provide a cosier feel. They are particularly suitable for large hall or stairwell areas to highlight objects of interest and to provide a bright source of light.

All three types of lighting should be as flexible as possible. Living rooms will need attractive as well as functional lighting. As with power points in kitchens, you may find you need more lighting than you originally thought, so allow for this when making a lighting plan.

LIGHTING IN PRACTICE

There are various ways of supplying the different types of lighting. Background illumination can be provided by lighting concealed behind pelmets, subdued lighting incorporated in display shelves, ceiling light fittings, a centrally placed pendant, recessed ceiling fittings or illuminated panels in the ceiling. Lighting can be concealed behind coving or cornice. It can be bounced off the ceiling by uplighters or lamps, wall lights, recessed fixtures set into floor, wall or ceiling or uplighters positioned to illuminate and shine through glass-topped tables or plant stands.

Direct lighting can be supplied by table, floor or desk lamps, spotlights trained on a particular area, fluorescent, incandescent tubes or circular fittings, strip lights or bulbs positioned above or round a mirror. It can also be provided by downlighters strategically positioned over baths, basins or sinks or wall-mounted light fittings over a bed.

Decorative or accent lighting is usually provided by spotlights. These can be individual, or several of them mounted on a ceiling or wall-mounted track, wallwashers, pinhole or framing projectors, uplighters and downlighters. Even candles can provide accent lighting.

Some fittings can perform several functions, and give a more flexible arrangement in a room where the lighting may have to be limited to a few different sources. In the initial stages, try to take as practical an approach to lighting as possible, seeing it as both functional and decorative.

Industrial lighting is worth considering. Curved and shaped tubes can be used to outline a picture or piece of sculpture, and a coloured neon tube can appear playful or daring in the right setting.

FIXTURES AND FITTINGS

Recent developments in the lighting industry have led to some confusion over the names and purpose of a wide variety of electrical equipment. The amount of light supplied by conventional sources and the wattage of light bulbs necessary for the different types of fitting vary, so check the information attached to any fittings you buy carefully.

Lighting specific items

You will not necessarily have something specific to display and illuminate in every room although a softly glowing light on display shelves, or a light shined on a curtain fabric to highlight the design can provide attractive background lighting. The accent lighting should be looked at in relation to the room as a whole, and each fitting should be individually controlled to avoid a glaringly bright effect when all the lighting is switched on at once.

Some objects, such as pieces of sculpture, require specialized lighting so that the shadows and interplay of light emphasize the form rather than detract from it. It may be necessary to experiment until you get exactly the right light. The

same may be true of a single object on a shelf, or a large single picture. It is possible to use lights with clips on a long cord to work out the best positions for any light fitting. If you have an extensive or very special or valuable collection of some type, it could be worthwhile calling in an expert lighting designer. In fact, if you want any specialized lighting for a conservatory or gallery, complicated exterior floodlighting for garden, patio and swimming pool, it may be wise to call in an expert, ideally at the planning stage.

To light a single picture or wall hanging, conventional picture lights are easy to install but tend to light only the top area of a large painting. Spotlights, either single and angled or mounted on

Lighting helps to create the atmosphere in this hall (right), which is used to display a collection of prints and paintings. The spotlights are trained to illuminate the pictures and mirror, but also to provide the background lighting to the hall as a whole. The dark-painted walls absorb light and act as a foil for the pictures.

track, work well but can cause glare on glass. Downlighters recessed in the ceiling above or uplighters placed below, can also give good illumination. For an excellent direct light, consider a framing projector. With a wall-hanging, where texture is all important, direct light can flatten and distort the effect. Try lighting it from the side, from below or above instead.

To light a group of pictures, the system may need to be different because there may be a larger wall area and possibly an unusual shape to consider. You may want to move or change the pictures from time to time, without upsetting the lighting pattern. A fitting such as a wall-washer fixed to the ceiling or behind a cornice or pelmet will flood the wall with light. Alternatively, use a row of downlighters or uplighters across the ceiling or floor or a track of spotlights angled right across the display area, fitted to the ceiling.

If you are lighting display shelves, try strip lighting above the shelves, concealed behind a cornice, pelmet or decorative arched moulding. Miniature or small eye-ball spotlights can be concealed amongst the shelves or they can be used singly or again mounted on a track above, below or to the side, and trained to show up items on the shelves. Downlighters and uplighters can also be used successfully, and if you actually place the objects inside a glass-fronted cabinet, the downlighters and uplighters can be tailored to fit inside also. Rows of tiny bulbs can be fitted across the top and bottom, down the sides or actually along the front edge of the shelves. Alternatively, these can be mounted on a miniature track, but take care not to use anything too clumsy. Glass shelves, for example, need to be very carefully lit and are better illuminated from above with concealed lighting or below with uplighting.

Lighting plants and flower arrangements is also important if they are to create impact and blend in with a room scheme at night. As flower arrangements are frequently changed, and plants do need moving around occasionally, the lighting must be flexible. One of the most effective ways of doing this is to stand the plants on a glass-topped table, and light them from below with an uplighter. This can create dramatic shadow effects on the walls and ceiling. If plants are large, conceal lighting amongst them. Any of the more conventional lighting methods can also be used. Keep some portable, adjustable lighting fixtures for lighting special flower arrangements.

1 Uplighters

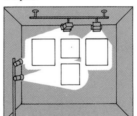

2 Spots

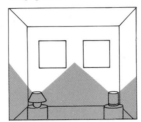

3 Fluorescent strips

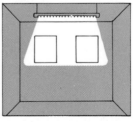

4 Picture lamps

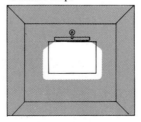

Lighting several objects in one area can be difficult. In this small drawing room setting (above), soft lighting bathes the bust with colour from a surface-mounted low voltage fitting with integral transformer. The table and plant are directly lit by a miniature low voltage fitting and the plant is also highlighted with an uplighter.

Pictures can be lit by directing lamps from beneath (1). Special uplighting units create an even, diffused light, spreading upwards and outwards.

Spotlights can be adjusted to create direct or reflected light (2). These can run on a special track, be ceiling mounted or hung below the ceiling. Single spots can be fixed to the wall, ceiling or floor or are available as free-standing units.

An arrangement of framed pictures can look best lit by one source. A strip of fluorescent lighting is ideal (3). Light can be directed on to the pictures by deflectors.

Individual picture lamps can be bought in a variety of sizes and shapes (4). A range of traditional and modern styles is available.

WAYS WITH WINDOWS

The window and the way in which it is dressed is an integral part of the interior decorating scheme. As with colour, pattern and texture, the selection of fabric and other materials, the style of window dressing will be influenced by the architecture of the room and the mood and atmosphere you are planning to create. It will also be affected by the type, size and shape of the window itself.

Large, opulent drapes, for example, with boldly swagged pelmet and 'tails' over lace panels, or delicate ruched blinds, look just right in big, bold windows in a traditional setting where there is plenty of space. Neat little café curtains, or crisp gingham-checked curtains with frilled edges and a ruched fabric valance are suitable for small windows in a cottage setting. Streamlined blinds or open-weave sheers are more suited to a modern environment.

Scale is important too. Big, bold patterns, bright colours and dramatic treatments look best on large windows or where there are several windows on one wall which can be unified by floor-to-ceiling and wall-to-wall curtains. A pattern which has been cut short at a small window will look odd. Check the pattern repeat (length from top to bottom) of any fabric you are buying and consider it in relation to the window and curtain drop. Plain fabrics with small patterns and less vibrant colours tend to work better at small windows.

When choosing fabrics and trimmings for a window, make sure they are fairly hard wearing. Fabrics need to be resistant to fading and shrinking and be able to stand up to strong sunlight and condensation.

The texture and type of fabric is important and must be considered in relation to the size and scale of the window and the style of the room scheme and furnishings. Satins, velvets, brocades, silks and taffetas, for example, will suit an elegant and more traditional setting, where the window dressing is a major part of the wall area. Lace, voiles, frilled net drapes and ruched blinds can give a bedroom a soft romantic atmosphere. Tweeds, grey flannel, severely-pleated Roman shades or streamlined venetians can be effective in a study or a modern living room.

APPROACHES TO WINDOWS

Combining window treatments can be practical and energy-saving. Roller, pleated, ruched, rattan, venetian or even insulated blinds can be combined with curtains, which can, in turn, be lined and interlined. This can prevent as much heat loss as double-glazing. Sometimes blinds are fixed close to the glass and the curtains simply act as a softly textured drape. They can be lace, net, or an open-weave sheer fabric. Closing the blinds at night under the curtains then gives extra privacy.

There are thousands of different types of fabric available for window dressing — woven, textured and printed, sheer and transparent. Make sure the scale is right for the window size. Small samples (below) are a good guide to colour and texture, but try to look at a full width and drop to judge the overall effect.

Where daytime privacy is essential, softly-draped sheer or net curtains, lace panels, café-style brise-bise nets, frilled jardinières, ruched or festooned sheer blinds can be combined successfully with heavier curtains. A roller blind fixed closed to the glass, or wooden or louvred shutters can also work well.

As alternatives to net curtains, use two tiers of café curtains or a roller blind which pulls up from the bottom. Both will let light in through the top part of the window.

Style coordination comes into its own in such multi-layer treatments. Plain curtains can be trimmed with a border or fringe to match the sheer drapes, nets can be edged with ribbon or trimmed with pleated floral frill to match the curtains. Roller blinds can be coordinated with the wallpaper, and combined with plain or patterned curtains.

Windows can be screened in different ways to give privacy and still let in the light. A panel of garden trellis, painted white or a soft pastel colour and tacked to a frame for ease of removal can help to hide an ugly view. Combined with an interesting selection of houseplants – some trained to climb the trellis – the effect will be extremely striking. Wrought-iron grilles can be used similarly and are good for security. Pierced hardboard panels can be treated to look like delicate filigree screens.

Stained glass is highly decorative. If you buy a house which already has some good glass, try to make a feature of it. If you have to close the curtains at night, make sure they are clear of the window during the daytime. If you want to use stained or other decorative glass to hide an ugly view, you can hang a panel inside the window (even better if it is sandwiched between two panes of glass), so you can enjoy the effect of light filtering through the coloured glass and throwing shadows onto the floor and walls. This is a flexible solution because you can take it with you if you move or put it into another room for a change of scene.

Stained glass effects can also be created by painting a design on a window with artists' inks or craft paint and simulating the leading.

Glass shelves fixed across the window reveal and used to display a collection of coloured glass, small objects or plants and herbs are another decorative treatment for a 'blind' window. You will need to choose hardy plants and double-glaze the exterior pane if this is to work effectively in winter. Try to illuminate the display at night with concealed lighting under a pelmet above a window, from uplighters below the sill or with spotlights.

Decorative bead curtains can also be used most effectively in the right setting to screen an ugly window or view. Some can be made up with a pictorial design, such as stylized flowers or leaves, be striped, checked or have some other more formal pattern.

Wooden internal shutters are sometimes found in older properties. They provide screening, security and extra insulation. They may have been screwed back, so that the side of the window frame looks as though it has wide panelling. It is worth investigating and unscrewing and repairing them where necessary. Blinds, net drapes, net café-style curtains can all be hung close to the glass. Shutters can be drawn across these at night, with perhaps an extra layer of floor-to-ceiling heavy drapes. Louvred panels can be used to replace or simulate

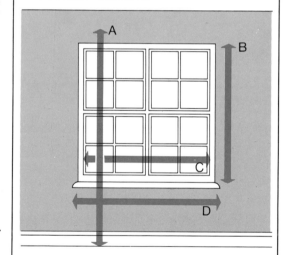

MEASURING WINDOWS

Windows must be measured accurately. Use a steel tape or wooden rule (fabric measures tend to stretch with use), and note down the measurements carefully.

Measure from the top of the window (or from the track or pole) to the floor (A) for floor-length curtains, or to the sill (B).

If you are measuring for blinds or café curtains to fit inside the window reveal, measure the inside edge of the window frame (C). Measure the width of the window, or the length of the track or pole if you intend to take the curtains past the edge of the frame (D).

shutters, and make a very attractive window treatment in their own right.

Make an alcove of an unused window – remove window handles and catches, face the back and build shelves across it (see page 155). Where the is a dark, blank area of wall in a corridor, hall, or perhaps on the turn of the stairs, you can create the illusion of a window. Pin up beading to form a frame or use a real window frame, and either paint a view on the wall behind, or glaze the false window with mirror. You can complete the image with lighting, curtains and an interior window box.

SELECTING THE RIGHT TREATMENT

It can sometimes be difficult to judge how a certain window treatment will look, and how effective it will be as part of a room scheme. One way of assessing results is to make elevated plans of the window walls to scale (see page 13), draw the

window to scale on the plan, and then sketch or pin on various styles until you achieve the correct balance. Alternatively use overlays made of tracing paper, tissue paper or transparent acetate. If this seems too fiddly or you find visually scaling up the plan difficult, you can make templates for pelmets, swags and tails, valances and other drapes from brown paper. Make these actual size and pin them to the top of the window frame to judge the effect. This will also help you to judge the depth of a pelmet and the length of curtains.

Apart from selecting the right fabric or other material and deciding on the correct style for the room, the actual choice of window treatment is also determined by the type and shape of the actual window. In one house alone you may find ten or more different styles of window, and some of them may well present problems requiring clever decorating and dressing techniques.

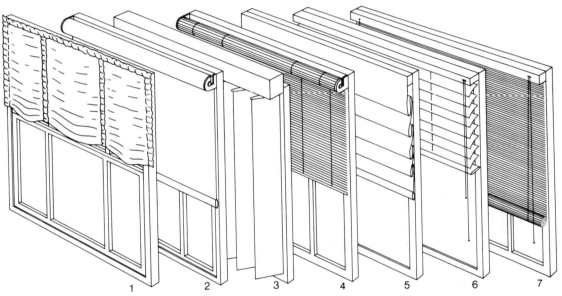

1 2 3 4 5 6 7

Blind line-up from left to right: Festoon or Austrian sheers (1) are softly draped, and drawn up with curtain-heading tape sewn vertically down the fabric at intervals. Sheer fabric is most suitable for this treatment. Roller blinds (2) come in a wide range of colours and patterns, in a stiffened fabric which is usually treated to shrug off dirt. If you make your own,

choose a stiffish, smooth fabric, which is not too bulky or textured. The roller has a retractable ratchet so the blind rolls up automatically.
Vertical venetian blinds (3) come with different slat widths, and in different textured fabrics, metal, plastic or wood. They can be ordered to pull to left or right, or to open in the centre.
Pinoleum blinds (4) are

made from narrow strips of rattan, and usually come in natural colours. although some are dyed to a rich colour, and some have had patterns printed or painted on them. In their classic green colour they are traditionally used in garden rooms and conservatories.
Roman blinds (5) are a flat pleated version of festoon blinds, and look neater and more tailored.

Venetian blinds (6) come in different slat widths, including fine blinds which give a similar see-through effect to sheer curtains. Stunning effects can be created by mixing the slat colours to make striped and bordered blinds. Bamboo blinds (7) are similar to pinoleum blinds, but are more chunky and have the characteristic texture of bamboo.

WINDOW TYPES

Arched windows are usually an attractive architectural feature. If so, try not to use curtains. If an arched window needs screening at night, floor-to-ceiling curtains will leave the window totally clear in the daytime. Alternatively, hang curtains from a pole positioned across the window at the point where the curve of the arch begins. A lace panel, nets or blinds hung from this point will provide daytime screening if required. As another option, curtains can be made with pleated headings to follow the curve of the window. This will have to be a permanent fixture, and the fall of the drape will have to be adjusted so that it hangs properly and is level at the floor. This type of drape needs to be fixed back with bosses or tie-backs.

Attic windows or roof lights may be sloping windows which are difficult to dress neatly (non-projecting dormers are different, see below).

Blinds can be fitted into new windows, with the blinds sandwiched between two panes of glass to act as double glazing. Venetian blinds can also be fitted with remote control if the window is high up. Roller blinds can be slotted into grooves parallel to the window frame with certain stop points, so that the blind can be adjusted. Alternatively hooks and eyes can be used. Roman blinds on a fixed track at the sides or curtain panels fixed at the bottom also work well. To prevent curtains falling forward on sloping windows, they can be fixed with a second pole. Suspend the curtains at the top with the first pole, and fix a second pole across the window at the angle of the slope. Make curtains extra-long so that they will be floor length when tucked behind the pole. Nets, lace or patterned sheers can be gathered and fixed at the top and bottom of a sloping window by expandable curtain wires threaded through the hem and heading. This treatment works best with lightweight fabrics.

Look at the basic window shape and decide whether it should be enhanced and emphasized, or disguised. Also consider the proportion — look at the size and shape of the window in relation to the room, and its position in the wall. You will also need to think about the window treatment style, which should echo the general furnishing and decorating theme and help to link the various surfaces with the furniture.

The window dressing, however simple, should never be treated as an afterthought or as an accessory — it should always be an integral part of the scheme. In fact, if patterned fabric is being selected for drapes, curtains or blinds, it could well be the starting point for a colour scheme.

Arched windows

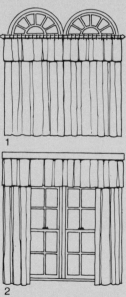

2

Arched windows can be very beautiful. If screening is essential, try tiers of café curtains which leave the arched tops visible (1). If necessary, unify with full-length curtains under a pelmet or valance (2).

Attic windows

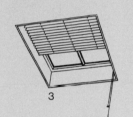

3

4

Attic windows are either sloping roof lights or dormer windows (see page 108). Roof lights can be fitted with special Venetian blinds (3) and are operated by remote control. For a softer look use curtains mounted on a pole (4), with a second pole at the angle of the slope.

Awning windows

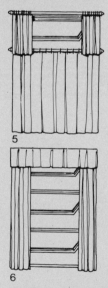

5

6

Awning windows are like louvred windows but the panes are larger and usually open outwards. For a tall awning window, try tiers of café curtains on rods which clear the window frame (5). For a more conventional setting, dress with curtains and pelmet or valance (6).

Awning windows usually open out horizontally and frequently come in rows, one above the other. Either fix curtains so they are well clear of the surround and the windows clear the curtains when open or fix curtains or blinds to the actual window pane frame so they move with the window. Try using tiered café-style curtains if several windows are above each other. The window opening can be fitted with louvred shutters or fabric insets, which are closed while the windows are open, yet still permit ventilation.

Bay and bow windows can be square bay, angled bay or curved 'bow'. Some are combined with deep window sills or window seats, making long curtains impractical unless the window can be completely enclosed at night. Track fittings following the line of the window can be concealed under a pelmet or valance. Poles are another possible solution.

If a fitted window seat is to be used at night, have floor-to-ceiling curtains each side of the bay or bow and fitted blinds to the sill coordinated with the seat cushions. Alternatively fit short curtains under the long ones.

If the window needs screening for privacy during the day, combine long or short curtains with nets or blinds. The nets can be café-style, or café curtains can be fitted halfway up the window pane either combined with a top tier or with long or short curtains. Cross-over net drapes also suit this type of window. In a modern scheme vertical blinds can be combined with curtains at the sides. An alternative to curtains if the window is not overlooked is a festooned pelmet in light fabric. This treatment will also soften the frame.

Casement windows are frequently small and may be fitted with leaded lights or diamond panes which tend to cut down the light. Some are double-sided, others are single, and they can swing in or outwards. With the in-swing type, the curtains have to clear the window to enable it to be opened and closed. Short curtains which draw neatly to each side fitted under a valance or pelmet work well, as the pelmet holds them away from the glass and frame. Hanging curtains on a pole also projects them into the room slightly. Café-style curtains, nets, shirred nets and blinds can all be mounted on the actual frame. This is a very practical treatment for in-swing casement windows.

Bay and bow windows

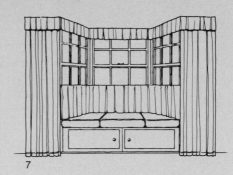
7

8

Bay and bow windows can be squared off, angular or gently curving. A window seat can be an attractive addition to an angular bay (7) with false curtains to each side of the window. The window can be partially screened with nets. Full-length drapes, combined with short sheers are a classic treatment for a bay (8).

Casement windows

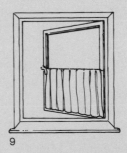
9

Casement windows are usually small and open outwards. Choose either small-scale pattern or plain fabric and keep the treatment neat. The window itself can be fitted with sheers, blinds or café curtains, which swing in or out with the window (9). For a softer look have short, full curtains under a frilled or pleated valance, which clear the window frame during the daytime (10).

10

A decorative frame for a small out-swing casement window lets in maximum light, but softens the frame. This idea can work extremely well for a window which does not need screening. Fabric on small casement windows should either be plain or have a small, neat pattern.

Clerestory windows are triangular in shape. They may be on their own but are more usually mounted above another window or patio door. Vertical venetian blinds are made to cope with a slope, and so can cover the whole window. In some cases curtaining or dressing the bottom part of the window and leaving the wedge above untreated is best. A tapered valance, pelmet or softly gathered net drape can echo the line of the top area and looks extremely elegant where a more traditional look is required.

Dormer windows are usually found at the top of the house just under the roof, and may have sloping flanking surrounds. The windows are flat but usually project out and tend to let in very little light. Short curtains or blinds in almost any style look good, and the space below the sill can often be filled with a built-in desk, dressing table, window seat or suitable piece of furniture. For a more elegant treatment hang floor-length, cross-over net drapes over a blind, or alternatively soft fabric, full length curtains, held in place with tie-backs. Where dormer windows have arched tops it may be necessary to combine one of these suggestions with an arched-top treatment.

French windows or doors can sometimes be unattractive in design, and a soft treatment makes them look more elegant. If they are flanked by short windows on each side, they can be unified with sheers or blinds – roller, venetian, roman or festooned – on the doors and to the sill on each window combined with floor-to-ceiling and wall-to-wall heavy drapes. Alternatively use vertical blinds (made of fabric) or vertical venetians (made of metal) right across the opening. Single or double French doors, without side windows, can be treated as tall windows or they can be fitted with net drapes, blinds or festoons fixed to the frame – unless you have a spectacular daytime view and are not overlooked – and combined with curtains or vertical venetians. These treatments can also be adapted to glazed front doors with side windows and very large picture windows.

Jalousie or louvred windows are made from narrow strips of glass and are opened by a crank or handle so that they can be angled. As they do not open inward or outward, but within their own frame, they can be treated in almost any way to suit the style of the room, bearing in mind that the glass strips jut out when in a fully open position. They can represent a security hazard – one strut is easy to cut and remove – so you might consider fitting inner shutters.

Narrow, tall windows seldom come in singles, except on a landing or in a hall and it is more usual to find two or three on one wall. The best treatment is to unify them with full-length curtains, which clear to each side of each window during the day, and form a continuous wall of fabric at night. If you

Clerestory windows

Dormer windows

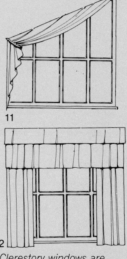

11

12

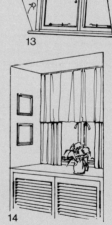

13

14

Clerestory windows are modern, sloping windows, often made up of a square or rectangle, with a triangle above set near the ceiling. If you want to drape this type of window softly, use a sheer or lightweight fabric, permanently fixed at the top and held back in the daytime with a tie-back (11). To unify this type of window, square off the top with a pelmet or valance and hang conventional curtains (12).

Dormer windows usually let in very little light. A simple roller blind (13) which retracts neatly during the daytime will let in maximum light. For a softer look, try tiers of café curtains, which can be made from a sheer fabric or lace (14). Cross-over net drapes can also look good in this situation.

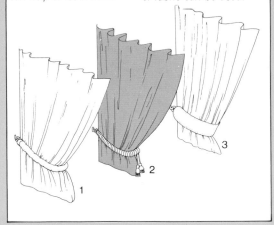

Tie-backs are used to hold the curtains in soft folds during the daytime, and can help to let in more light if they hold the curtains back clear of the frame. Cord, fringe, ribbon or fabric can be used.

want to make them appear shorter, choose fabric with a horizontal pattern, or make two or three tiers of café curtains. On one narrow window, take the track right past the frame, so that the curtains are fuller and clear the frame during the day and the window looks wider. Narrow, tall windows can also be combined on one wall with other shaped windows, and as with French doors, the secret of design success is to unify them.

Oriel windows are usually found in eighteenth-century-style properties and are so beautiful in their own right it is a shame to cover them with curtains. If it is absolutely essential to screen them for privacy, take the curtain track well past the frame to allow the curtains to clear the windows. Otherwise treat them as bays.
bays.

French windows

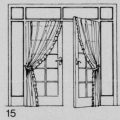

15

16

French windows are full-length versions of the casement window and usually open outward, but they can be used as internal, inward-opening doors. Double doors can be treated individually with drapes fitted to the frame (15), or cross-over net drapes can be used. A shirred valance looks attractive above French windows (16), with full-length curtains which pull to each side during the day.

Jalousie windows

17

18

Jalousie or louvred windows are narrow, horizontal strips of glass, which open by crank within their own frame, to provide angled ventilation. The entire window can be treated as one (17), with a neat valance or pelmet and short café curtains. For a more flexible treatment which ensures privacy, fit curtains or fabric inserts to the frame (18). This is particularly suitable if there is a bank of several louvred windows on one wall.

Narrow, tall windows

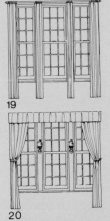

19

20

Narrow, tall windows can be made to seem shorter, by combining full-length curtains to each side, with short café curtains which come about halfway up the glass (19). A group of narrow, tall windows on one wall can be unified with a pelmet or valance with curtains pulled to each side during the daytime. This works well if the windows are elegant, using the area of wall between the central windows to display pictures or 'objets d'art' (20).

Oriel windows

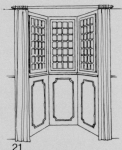

21

Oriel windows can be very elegant and are best left unscreened. They may be combined with a window seat in some circumstances, in which case they can be treated as a bay or bow window (see page 107). Net panels, cane, rattan and other pierced screens can soften this type of window by filtering light softly through. If curtains are essential for privacy, try to close the whole window off at night with floor-to-ceiling drapes (21).

Ranch windows are short, wide and sometimes have sliding panes. They are found in ranch-style properties and are usually placed high up in the wall. They can be dressed to make them appear longer and less wide. Long curtains can be used unless the window is situated high up. Do not use a pelmet or valance with curtains, as this tends to overemphasize the width. A good method is to suspend the curtains from poles or track with possibly a false pelmet or valance above the window to make it appear taller. Alternatively, a scalloped or awning-style canopy could be fitted above the window.

Sash windows are widely found in older properties. They slide open up and down and generally look best with a bold, elegant treatment if they are part of a distinctive period-style setting. Opulent drapes in heavy fabrics with impressive pelmets, swags and tails, or festoons to top them will have this effect, or you can use curtains with pleated or other dramatic headings, suspended on poles. Floor-length curtains suit sash windows and if combined with another covering the inner layer can be floor length or just to the sill. Where two

sash windows appear on one wall they can be dressed in a unified way, or you can attract attention to the space in between by making curtains on the two windows which pull to the edge of each frame and place a picture, mirror or other decorative item on the wall between the two windows, or some houseplants on a stand.

Patio doors and picture windows are usually large, often a whole wall of window, and patio doors slide open or open out. Picture windows are not necessarily floor-length, they can sometimes be landscape in shape and open like casement windows, as well as sliding. Patio doors are the modern equivalent of French doors and can be treated in a similar way. Quite often they let in so much light and sun it is essential to have some sort of screen fitted under the curtains. Pleated, solar filter blinds which are transparent and diffuse light, cutting out harmful rays are available. Curtains should be floor-to-ceiling length on both patio doors and picture windows, and from wall-to-wall. Pull them back to clear as much of the window as possible during the daytime to avoid fading the fabric at the sides.

Ranch windows

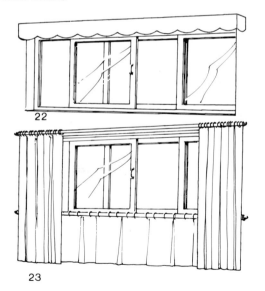

22

23

A draped canopy across the top will soften ranch windows (22). Add side drapes, which are suspended from a pole, going past the edge of the frame. Suspend café-style curtains beneath on a matching pole — these can be longer than sill length to help create the illusion (23).

Sash windows

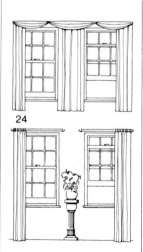

24

25

Sash windows look best with an important elegant treatment. Combine full-length curtains with pelmet, swags and tails or valance (24). Two together on a wall can be treated as tall, narrow windows (25).

Patio doors

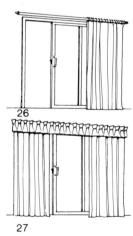

26

27

Patio doors often slide within their frames. Use floor-to-ceiling drapes and pull the curtains to one side for easy access (26). For a more formal room, use valance or pelmet and full-length drapes to each side (27).

For all curtain styles floor-length curtains should just clear the floor to prevent abrasion. Sill-length curtains should be exactly that, just to the sill and not hanging limply a few inches below. When the curtains have been washed or cleaned, the length may need adjusting. Allow for this when making curtains or having them made up.

DECORATING DIFFICULT WINDOWS

If you are faced with difficult windows, you can play tricks with window dressing which will deceive and please the eye.

Awkward corner windows usually come in pairs, and fit either side of a corner. Try to unify them with the window treatment. If the outlook is pleasant, hang curtains so that they pull back to the left and right, leaving all the glass clear. If the windows are tall, hang nets or blinds down to the sill with full-length curtains each side, unified at the top with a pelmet or festoon drapery. Café curtains look attractive when combined with a window seat.

If the window has no view, roller blinds with an interesting pattern or a painted 'view' can be fitted and kept closed. If you need the window to provide a source of light, hang a blind which rolls up from the bottom, a sheer roller blind, a lace panel or sheer vertical blinds. Fine-slatted venetian blinds let in a surprising amount of light when slightly opened.

Make a narrow window look wider by hanging curtains or draperies well over to each side of the frame – take track or pole beyond the window edge.

Make a wide window look narrower by keeping the curtains together at the top, and draped back softly at the sides with tie-backs.

Make a short window look taller by fixing the track well above the frame, and combining it with a dominating heading like a shaped pelmet, canopy or pleated or smocked valance. Make the curtains floor length or have several tiers of café curtains.

Make a small window look bigger by hanging tiers of café curtains.

Make a tall window look shorter by putting up a deep pelmet, the top of the pelmet flush with the top of the window box, preferably with an interesting shape, and hanging short curtains.

Awkward corner windows

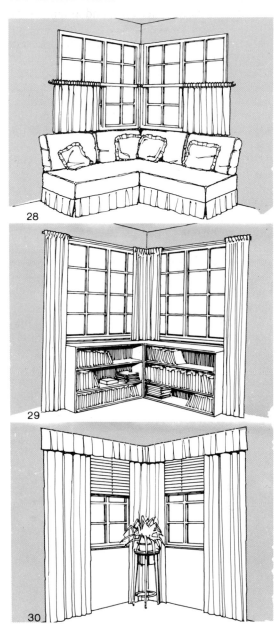

28

29

30

Awkward corner windows look better when unified. For an informal look, use café curtains on rods right into the corner — one or several tiers depending on window height (28).

Furniture fitting into the corner (28, 29) can help link the two windows, but floor-length curtains to each side can be false, with shorter curtains to the sill providing the screen.

Blinds combined with full-length curtains will allow heat to circulate from radiators (30).

METHODS OF SUSPENSION

The style of curtain you select will determine the means of suspension and the type of heading the curtains need. If the curtains are to hang from a curtain or cornice pole, this will be mounted on brackets above the window frame, and pleated curtain headings can form a decorative part of the overall look. There are various ways of pleating headings (see below right), and poles can either be fitted with rings or have gliders concealed in the lower edges of the pole. The curtains can be headed with tape, and conventional hooks used to slip into the gliders or the special eyes in the rings. Alternatively, round rings can be sewn on to the back of each pleat in the curtain heading and these can be passed over the pole, or hooks can be threaded through and into the gliders. Pleated headings can also be combined with a sleek neat curtain track which is designed to be seen.

If the curtains are to be fitted with pelmets or valances at the top, they can have a simple, gathered heading as it will not be seen. Pelmets are fixed to the tops of curtains by means of a pelmet board. Valances need a special double track, one part for the curtain to move along and the other part for the valance. Both curtains and valance are fixed to the track by means of hooks, slipped through the heading, and passed through gliders on the track.

Café curtains are usually mounted on special rods or poles, which are then fixed to the window frame or mounted each side of it. The curtains can be headed in any of the conventional ways or they can be scalloped. Some special nets, sold for café curtains, (brise-bise) have special casings through which the rod can pass.

Neat, slimline track, which is usually fixed to the top of the window frame, will come complete with gliders. Hooks in the heading tape then fix the curtains to the track. Shirred curtains and some net drapes are fixed to the window frame by special extending wire, although they can also be fixed by a narrow rod. The curtains either have a casing at the top, and sometimes bottom edge as well, or the wire or rod is slipped through a hem. Nets and sheers can also be headed like conventional curtains, although special 'invisible' heading tape needs to be used, and then pleated or gathered. They can be suspended by means of poles or track.

Curtain panels may cover the entire window or be made to café curtain length and require two hems top and bottom which take either wooden or

Pinch pleats gather the fabric up crisply and look decorative (1). Pencil pleats form neat, regular folds and need a lot more fabric (about three times the track width) (2). Triple pinch pleats give a fuller curtain than single or double pleats, but allow a softer drape than pencil pleating (3). Tops can be scalloped or lace/sheers clipped into rings on a rod (4).

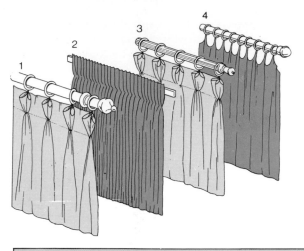
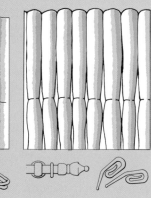
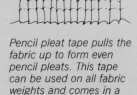

TAPES AND TRACKS
Cartridge pleat tape

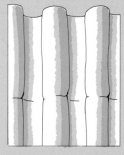
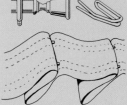

Pencil pleat tape

Cartridge pleat tape pulls up the curtains into evenly-spaced rounded cartridge pleats. It is particularly good with heavyweight fabrics such as velvets and brocades.

Pencil pleat tape pulls the fabric up to form even pencil pleats. This tape can be used on all fabric weights and comes in a variety of widths. Between $2\frac{1}{4}$ and $2\frac{1}{2}$ times the track length of fabric is needed for this tape.

brass poles. The top pole is attached by hooks at either side while the bottom pole hangs free to keep the panel uniformly flat. If attached to a slanting attic window the bottom pole should also be attached.

Commercially made curtain panels have their own means of mounting and suspension and may be electrically operated to slide open or closed.

Tracks and poles are also available for special treatments. If you want to fix a curtain behind a door, for example, to prevent catching it each time the door is opened or closed, you will need a special portière rod which rises and falls as the door opens. Curtains for dividers can be fixed to the ceiling by means of ceiling-mounted track, sometimes actually embedded in the ceiling, poles, cubicle curtain track or rods. All blinds come complete with their own means of mounting and suspension.

A suitable way of fixing curtains in a modern scheme where curtains run wall to wall, is by attaching a wire tautly at either end of the wall and running the wire through eyelet holes at the top of the curtain.

Softly gathered valance, combined with tied-back curtains (1). Box-shape pelmet, which is usually preformed. It can be covered with fabric or wallpaper to match the scheme or painted (2). Shaped pelmet is usually made from fabric stiffened with buckram (3). Drapable fabric or nets and sheers can be softly gathered to form a fall of fabric at the side of the frame, and combined with café curtains or blinds (4).

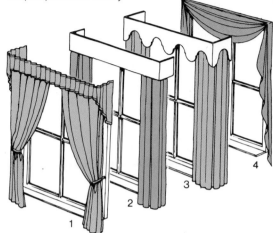

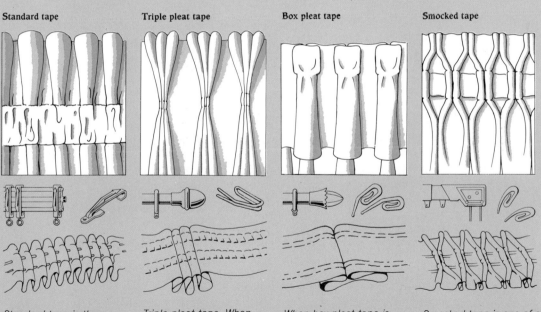

Standard tape

Standard tape is the simplest and cheapest form of heading tape. It merely gathers the fabric. Use it under pelmets or in kitchens and bathrooms. It looks best with lightweight, unlined curtains.

Triple pleat tape

Triple pleat tape. When stitching this tape, work from where the curtains will meet outwards so that the groups of pleats are evenly spaced and the curtain tops match across each curtain.

Box pleat tape

When box pleat tape is pulled up, the curtain top folds into evenly-spaced box pleats. Because of the pleat width this works well with heavier, lined curtains. You will need roughly 2½ times the track length of fabric.

Smocked tape

Smocked tape is one of a range of decorative heading tapes, which cleverly gives the fabric top a smocked effect. it is most suited to sheer fabrics but can be used on most other curtaining fabrics.

SECTION THREE

DESIGN RECOVERY

Your interior design problem may not require a complete scheme change, it may simply be a matter of minor alteration. Ugly pipes, an unattractive fireplace surround, a dull or dark colour scheme, or garish bathroom tiles are all minor problems, but they can spoil the overall look of a room. Different solutions designed to suit different styles are described and illustrated in this trouble-shooting section. A room can sometimes just feel wrong for no apparent reason - flicking through this section may help you identify the cause of the problem as well as show you how to rectify it with a minimum of fuss. Even if your particular problem is not included here, you will probably find a solution to it among the wealth of suggestions for concealing, disguising and enhancing different features.

Renovation may not be something you would consider undertaking yourself, but it is useful to know what will be involved in, for example repairing plasterwork. Experts may suggest more drastic refurbishment than is absolutely necessary, and this section outlines the alternatives. It looks at problem structural surfaces which may have to be dealt with before redecoration is started. Ways of disguising poor ceilings and walls, levelling uneven floors, choosing doors and renovating decrepit staircases are all suggested.

The section on camouflage deals with problems of proportion. Simple visual illusions can transform a room with colour and pattern, for example, making a high room seem lower, blending projections and recesses into the background or even creating interest in a boring, box-shaped room.

SOLVING IN-BUILT PROBLEMS

When you look at your home with a view to decorating it or reworking an existing scheme, you will probably find that its attractive features are offset by other, less pleasing, characteristics. Some properties are just badly designed. Others simply have minor irritations like three windows of different shapes on one wall; obtrusive fireplaces; or unattractive but practical built-in furniture and dark corridors, halls and landings, sometimes cluttered with pipes and cables. All these problems can be dealt with and some of the solutions are surprisingly simple.

If you have recently moved home, you may find it difficult to fit in your existing furniture, curtains, carpets and accessories so that they blend with the new environment and the existing decorations. There are also self-inflicted problems when decorating. A wall covering, flooring or upholstery fabric can be the right colour and look superb in the shop, but just does not work when it is up on the wall or down on the floor. Units and worktops can also cause problems – they often do not look the same in reality as they did in the catalogue or shop. Or you may find once you have completed your decorating scheme, that you are left with an over-garish or boring room.

If such disheartening problems do arise, look at the room or particular difficulty as critically and clinically as possible – it may help to pretend that you are not dealing with your own home, but rather a situation which you are trying to solve professionally. If this proves difficult, ask a neighbour, friend or member of the family for an unbiased opinion. You may be surprised at how quickly the right solution springs to mind, or indeed how many possible solutions there are.

PIPES

You certainly cannot dispense with the plumbing, but visible pipes can be an eyesore. They are most likely to occur in older properties, where thoughtless replanning, replumbing or conversion

work has gone on over the years. Basement corridors and hall or landing areas are particularly prone to these problems. Kitchens and bathrooms can also suffer from too many pipes.

Solving the problem

A very simple solution is to wallpaper over the pipes using a paper with a striking pattern. The pipes are then hardly noticeable. Alternatively you can leave some exposed and paint them to match the overall colour of the wallpaper or use any of the paint techniques such as spattering, marbling or sponging. These work particularly well if the walls and skirtings are treated similarly. You might wish to make a feature of the pipes, by painting them in strong, contrasting primary colours. For a more traditional look, paper behind the pipes with a busy pattern. Pick out the pipes in one or more of the colours in the paper.

Boxing in the pipes is another option, as long as accessible inspection hatches are included. Boxing-in is practical and can be made almost invisible if you paint it to match the wall or skirting

board or by using a little *trompe l'oeil.* You can also adapt basic boxwork to match other fittings in a room. Overlapping one side of a corner box makes an alcove for small shelves. Backed by mirror tiles the illusion is created that the shelves run from the front to the back of the wall. An upstanding front edge on horizontal pipework can be doubled up as a planter – you can even make the box large enough for standard plant pots or troughs. The boxwork can then be painted or covered in cork.

For a fun solution and informal appearance, wrap the pipes in coloured lagging and tie it in place with a cross-gartering of ribbons. This 'leg-warmer' technique will also insulate the pipes.

A 'rainbow' solution can be effective where a lot of pipes run side-by-side. Paint them in a spectrum of different colours, starting at the top with red, and working down through orange, yellow, green, blue and violet. If this will not blend with your colour scheme or suit the style of the room, use pastel versions of these colours, or graded values of one colour – start at the top with the lightest tone or shade, and work down.

If you can't beat 'em, join 'em! Here obtrusive pipes have become part of the High tech kitchen scheme. The lighting track and spotlights form a frame over the cooking/serving area and encompass pipes (left).

Air conditioning can be obtrusive as in this relaxing/sitting area (right). *If a large unit like this is essential, make a feature of it by painting in a bold accent colour.*

RADIATORS

Central heating is widely used in cold climates but the sources of heat vary. Conventional or old-fashioned upright radiators are likely to be at best noticeable or at worst, dominate the whole room. Siting can be wrong too - many radiators, for example, are placed under the main window, causing a great deal of heat loss. In some rooms this positioning makes fitting in the furniture difficult, especially where the ideal place for a desk, work or play surface, dressing table, bath, sink, or window seat would be under the window.

Solving the problem

Change the position - or change the type of heat supply if you really do not have room for a radiator. Skirting heating can be run off an existing central heating system and looks neat, even elegant, in some situations. It can be combined with fitted furniture, or mounted on a plinth (the heating running along the plinth) and with full-length curtains. The heat output, however, tends to be low.

Wall-mounted heating or air conditioning can often be practically sited - mounted on a disused chimney breast, in a fireplace surround, highly placed above units, incorporated in a wall of shelves or mounted between cupboards.

Treat the radiator decoratively so that it fades into the background. Either paint it to match the surrounding wall area or paint it to match the background of the wall covering behind it. Never treat a radiator as though it were part of the woodwork or 'trimmings' to a room. You can also incorporate the radiator in an integral, striking design. Paint the wall with an interesting pattern - clouds, waves, a rainbow, or perhaps in an angular 'graphic' way - and then continue the design on to the surface of the radiator.

In the right situation - a child's room, playroom, games room or secondary area (like the downstairs lavatory) - make a feature of the radiator. Give it flamboyant treatment so that it really stands out. It can be painted in bold colours to look like a flag, decorated to look like a sheep, zebra, tiger or other favourite animal or made to look like a train, car, caravan or ship, if the room has a definite theme of that kind. You can make it thoroughly decorative with garlands of flowers, or give it the 'bargeeware' treatment with formal flower sprigs in green, red and white on a coloured background.

Radiators can be treated as an integral part of the decorating scheme, so they fade into the background or as an attractive item in their own right. If you want to merge a radiator with the background, paint it to match the surrounding wall area and not to match the woodwork.
In the bathroom (above) the radiator has been used as the divider between the bathroom and bedroom areas. It is in keeping with the 1930s style of the house and adds a characteristic charm to the room.
The elegant brass grille (top right) conceals the presence of a radiator completely.
The hall radiator (centre right) is attractively marbled to match the wall behind, and consequently melts into the background.
In the kitchen/dining area (right) a modern Runtal radiator is used to screen the dining area from the food preparation section of the room.

Replace the existing radiator with a more attractive model. Facsimiles of old-fashioned designs which stand on the floor against the wall are available. There are other individual designs of elegant shape and finish, with basic styles sufficiently adaptable to fit comfortably into a variety of schemes for décor and furnishing. Alternatively there are now some modern designs which look almost like wall sculptures and which are available in a vast range of colours to enliven a more contemporary scheme.

Box in a radiator if you want a secret solution to suit an elegant room. Either include a grille of brass or another metal so that the heat can still circulate or conceal the radiator with a wooden grid or trellis, either natural or painted, to suit the chosen scheme. In the right situation in a bow or bay window or where there is a deep reveal, you can combine this treatment with a window seat.

Blend in the radiator if it comes under a window sill and there is space at each side of the window. Have vertical venetian blinds made, with a space cut-out in the middle. This cut-out is made by combining short and long slats – the long slats coming to either side of the window frame, and the short ones to the sill. This treatment can be even more effective if the slats are in two or three contrasting or toning colours and the radiator is striped in paint to match.

If the window is very attractive and the radiator is not very high, of course, the window dressing can be a problem (see some solutions on pages 102 to 113). Where you do not need curtains, paint the window frame and the radiator in a strong colour, and dress the window with a pictorial roller blind. Pictorial blinds can be bought ready made or ordered to your own design.

Divert attention from the radiator. Position a shelf along the top, mounted on brackets clear of the top of the radiator, and display an eye-catching collection of objects or plants. Again paint the shelf and radiator to match the basic wall colour. Take this idea a stage further and use the whole wall area for a complete run of shelves, incorporating the radiator.

If several radiators are sited on a long wall, paint them to match the background. Hang large pictures framed to the same size as the radiators above each one and light with a spotlight.

FIREPLACES

With the efficiency of modern heating systems, fireplaces are used less often for open fires. Open fires are still, nevertheless, a popular feature and are often included in modern houses. In older properties, you may find that the fireplace and surround are not in pristine condition. In both modern and older houses, the fireplace may simply be extremely ugly. There are various ways of converting a fireplace to make it either into an attractive focal point or to make it unobtrusive so that it blends in with the room without the inconvenience of taking it out. Taking out a fireplace is a possibility, but it can be heavy work.

Solving the problem

Enhance the surround by painting it to contrast with the wall area or use one of the specialist painting techniques, such as marbling, tortoiseshelling or rag rolling. A good-looking wood surround may have had countless layers of paint applied over the decades and stripping the paint and waxing the wood will transform it. You may find when you strip the surface that the surround is made of marble and not wood. Test a small area on the underside of the mantlepiece, because some proprietary wood strippers are not suitable for use on marble, and will damage the surface.

Install some attractive fittings if the fireplace is to be used for an open fire. Choose a style in keeping with the surround and with the décor of the room, if necessary bridging the gap with new tiles of marble, stone or brick. Consider fitting a wood or multi-purpose fuel-burning stove within the fireplace opening.

Disguise the surround if it is not particularly interesting but you do not want to remove it. Decorate it to match the background, so that the fireplace merges into the wall. Make an eye-catching arrangement in the recessed spaces by installing shelves, perhaps above low cupboards, with arched alcoves. Hang a bold picture, wall-hanging or other focal point on the wall above the fireplace, but never put a mirror above a fireplace which is being used as there might be a safety risk involved. If the fireplace is not used, however, mirror tiles, arranged in a striking pattern above the fireplace, can be attractive.

The fireplace (above) needs considerable refurbishment, but is basically attractive.
If the surround is attractive, you can remove the old tiles, hearth and grate, and install a wood-, gas- or multi-fuel-burning stove (below left). *An attractive design can become a focal point. The*

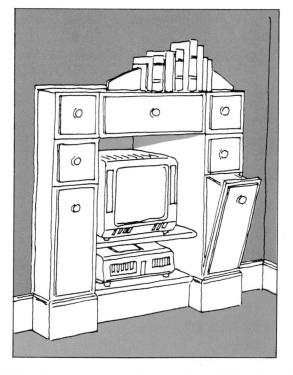

Convert the interior part of the fireplace, leaving the surround in place. It can make an attractive alcove and be used for many purposes. It can house a television set or stereo equipment, or become a small built-in cupboard or open bookcase.

If you want to make a dramatic focal point of the area, put concealed lighting into the recess, back it with a mirror, or mirror tiles, and display a collection of plants, flower arrangement, china or glass objects. Glass shelves could also be installed across the recess and small, decorative items be displayed.

If you decide to cut out most of the breast, but have to leave the two supporting walls, you can be more adventurous with built-in furniture, making larger cupboards and bigger shelves.

Rearrange the furniture to conceal the fireplace. In a bedroom, for example, the bed can be placed against the chimney breast, and the fireplace surround might act as a bed-head. The chimney

breast might be incorporated into a dressing-table design. In a dining area, storage units or free-standing furniture of different depths can be selected, some filling the recesses, the narrower ones butting up to the breast and all fitting flush at the front. In a sitting area, a sofa can conceal an unsightly fireplace. A folding screen of wood or painted panels can provide a good temporary disguise, or even a long wall-hanging or rug can do the trick.

Cover up the noticeable features. Sometimes you can just remove the mantlepiece and clad the entire wall area of the breast and sides and possibly the alcoves with wood cladding mounted on battens, stone, brick, slate or other materials.

Choose a cladding which is in keeping with the architectural style of the property and is not too overpowering. A vast stone or brick chimney breast would be far too dominating in a small modern house or modest cottage, for example.

opening can be filled with storage units to taste (below centre). Here we show a television and video unit, with storage for video tapes, discs and

casettes in pull-out and drop-down sections. Adapt the surround (below right). Install lights as an integral part, fill the fireplace opening with a

louvre-fronted storage cupboard, and include a drop-down, triangular flap table.

This unusual sloping ceiling in an attic bathroom (left) could create a cramped and oppressive feel. The light treatment for walls, woodwork and sloping beams and sanitary ware, make the area seem lighter and taller.

The light but warm wall treatment, with white bedlinens graphically checked in yellow (below), gives a small dark bedroom the light touch. A whole wall of mirror panels brings in more light making the room seem brighter and more spacious. In a bedroom the bedlinens are a large part of the exposed surface and the choice of colour and pattern can make or mar a scheme.

DARK ROOMS

Dark ground floor rooms need a light touch. Sometimes when two rooms are knocked into one, one end can seem dark and dismal. Or when an extension or conservatory is added, it can reduce the light from one or more rooms. Rapidly growing trees and hedges, projecting fences or walls and tall buildings can all create a similar problem.

Solving the problem

Use a mirror or a panel or wall of mirror tiles to provide reflected light. Test the position until you find the point where there is maximum reflection. In rooms with recessed walls a mirror can be positioned on the back wall of an alcove. Illuminate with concealed lighting or attractive uplighters for maximum night-time effect.

Decorate the room in sunshine colours of bright clear yellow and sparkling white or use sunset colours of orange, flame and gold with white.

Glaze or part-glaze doors. If this see-through look will interfere with privacy, put mirrors into the door panels instead or use frosted, coloured or patterned glass.

Remove heavy curtains from a window or garden door at the dark end of the room. Replace with floor-to-ceiling net or lace drapes, which can create an impression of light, and install a roller blind behind the drapes to create privacy when the room is lit at night. Alternatively, use a run of vertical venetians across the end wall. They are available in several bright colours as well as metallic finishes and let in a great deal of light when partially opened, at the same time ensuring privacy.

Make attractive displays of indoor plants, objects grouped on a glass-topped table, ornaments or sculpture or a well-displayed picture, and use uplighters, spotlights or, in the case of the picture, picture gallery lighting for illumination.

The heavy wooden furniture (below) appears lighter and more fragile because of the white framing.
Walls and ceiling in pastel peach add a soft sunshine touch, with a warmer glow echoed in the distinctive bedcover — the strong leaf pattern helps to draw the eye away from the heavy head and foot ends of the bed.

The diagonally painted cupboard (right) looks like an integral part of the room scheme. This bold treatment adds a bright touch and the mirrored door reflects the posters pinned to the adjacent wall, again helping to make the whole area seem brighter and more interesting. Warm autumnal colours echo the sunshine mood.

BUILT-IN FURNITURE

Built-in cupboards, units and furniture are often convenient, but they may be too bulky or obvious for the style of your rooms. Junk shop, jumble or garage sale finds can help to solve storage problems, but an old or dilapidated piece can seem really ugly or out of place in a well decorated room. However, built-in furniture can be dressed up to look elegant or tempered so that it merges with the surroundings. Treat the furniture in different ways, according to the décor and function of each room.

Solving the problem

Some types of built-in furniture can be cut down or structurally altered to change the shape of the unit. If you think it can, call in a carpenter. Sometimes bulky old furniture can be dismantled and made into several new pieces. An old, well-made wardrobe, for example, might break down into a bed base (the lower drawers) two cupboards, a wall-mounted mirror, and some open

shelves. An old hall stand can be divided up to make a wall-mounted clothes rack, a side table and an umbrella stand. A washstand might convert to a serving table and a wall-mounted mirror.

Look for potential in old but well-constructed items of furniture, but don't waste time and money on poorly-made pieces. Cheap veneered surfaces cannot be improved even by painting, but you may be lucky and find a beautiful solid wood carcass underneath layers of old paint.

Clad the doors of heavy built-in wardrobes with mirror tiles or sheets of mirror glass, making sure the frames and hinges can take the extra weight. This will make the furniture seem less obvious as well as magnifying the size of the room and providing some reflected light.

Paper the doors and drawer fronts to coordinate with the wall coverings and fabrics used in the room. Most wall coverings adhere easily to a cupboard door, but can curl up at the edges with constant handling. Take a paper or vinyl wall covering to within 2.5 cm/1 in of the edge of the door or drawer and hide the raw edges under decorative beading, pinned and/or glued in position.

Take the doors off altogether and replace them with colourful roller blinds for a lighter look or light and lacy fabric curtains.

Paint the whole unit in a fairly strong colour to match the rest of the décor. Paint and stain the panels and pin picture-frame beading or plain wooden edging around the panels in a contrasting colour. Pin simple wooden garden trellis with a diamond pattern to form panels on a plain area. Change handles or knobs to suit the new style.

Use specialist painting techniques to enliven the surface finish. Get out a paint brush or some sponges and rags, and necessary materials, and start experimenting with marbling, sponge-stippling, dragging, rag-rolling, combing, scumbling (simulating a highly decorative woodgrain) or tortoiseshelling. Soft, non-defined paint techniques create a feeling of space and translucency and amazing effects can be achieved.

Cans of spray paint are available in a wide range of colours and are easy to handle when painting small areas like door and drawer fronts.

When working on doors it is often best to take them off their hinges and lay them flat, to avoid smudges, runs and sags in the paint while you are working. Always take drawers out of furniture and work on them horizontally.

For a light look in a small bedroom with wood-clad walls, pull-down roller blinds are used instead of cupboard doors on the storage units (left). Heavy looking wood cupboards can be similarly treated — remove the doors and close the gap with blinds or vertical venetians, or use softly draped curtains.

Make an appliqué pattern or collage in a child's bedroom or playroom – paste on scrapbook material and varnish over it, or make a pattern with shapes cut from self-adhesive plastic. Cut templates from brown paper or newspaper first as self-adhesive materials can be difficult to alter once the backing is removed. Use this idea as a temporary measure to enliven ageing doors and drawers in the kitchen too.

Use a stencilled design to create an entirely new personality for storage units or furniture. Strip off the old surface if necessary, clean thoroughly and repaint. Stencil with traditional border patterns in classic style – Greek-key, dog's tooth or egg-and-dart. There are many border papers in these styles which you can use as a template for cutting stencils. Alternatively create a Delft-tile

look in blue and white, or an Etruscan effect with black and terracotta. Simulate bargee or Romany patterns with stencil or paint.

Paint a pattern on the doors, drawers, top and sides of the furniture. Carry the pattern over onto the wall behind and above or add touches that echo the design. You can use any of the ideas suggested for radiators (see page 118) or invent your own. Try a tree or jungle scene or a vista effect in a small, square room to add an extra dimension.

For total camouflage buy sheets of woven rattan or woodstrips intended for blinds, linen or hessian. Attach them to the furniture and cover the raw edges with split bamboo. Seal the entire surface against dust and dirt with a transparent seal or paint over for a more subtle textured effect.

A garden atmosphere is created in a small dining area (above), where a stencilled pattern on the wall area creates an impression of foliage and flowers. The line of the tree foliage has been designed so that awkward angles and corners in the room come forwards, almost flattening the projections.

A simple, but effective treatment (right) involves papering the panels of the wardrobe doors to match the walls, and edging with paint to hide any uneven joins.

ROOMS WITH NO VIEW

When you choose a home, you doubtless pay particular attention to the natural light coming into the main living areas and the view from the windows. But there may be some internal rooms, such as the bathroom and inner hall, that have no windows at all. The main rooms may also have a bleak prospect such as a window which looks out on to a wall. Landing windows can overlook the neighbouring property and windows high up in the recesses to each side of a chimney breast may let in some light but are often unattractive.

Solving the problem

Take out the old glass and replace it with stained glass in a design and style to suit the house, its furnishings and the overall decoration. There are many stained glass artists who work to commissions, but you can also find old stained glass panels in antique shops, glass merchants and some builders' yards. There are also special paints and 'leading' materials and waterslide transfers available for doing it yourself.

Display coloured glass against the window. This is another way of getting colourful light filtering through. Even simple, crudely designed bottles will do. Fix glass shelves across the reveal to take the collection – adjustable brackets are the most practical means of suspension.

Colour wash the glass with a single colour for an easy but effective solution to suit the décor of the room and produce a glowing light source.

Use soft furnishings imaginatively – a beautiful net panel, filmy voile drape or sheer woven fabric can act as a very pretty screen. Combine the fabrics with a blind hung close to the glass for night time privacy. A filmy festoon or ruched blind can also act as a fabric screen under heavier drapes (see pages 103 to 113 for more ideas).

Close off an ugly window with gridded screens. These can be made of rattan, pierced hardboard, wrought iron or other metals. Extremely effective screens can be made from screening material intended for use as room dividers or from simple garden trellis. Trellis can be mounted on a frame which exactly fits the window opening and looks particularly effective when house plants are trained to climb or to trail over it.

Decorative glass (below) can screen an ugly view, and provide visual interest in itself.

Create a conservatory image in a window (bottom), using glass shelves.

The pierced screen has been used to close off the bay window completely in this basement sitting area (above) where the view is a dismal one of area steps and dustbins. The Moorish atmosphere is echoed in the furnishings and accessories.

A hospital type folding fabric screen (right) is unfolded across this very small corner window in the evening and to provide privacy. When full light is needed, the screen is folded and placed to the side of the window.

PLAIN WALLS

A large expanse of blank wall can look stark and cold above the sofa in the living room or the bedhead in the bedroom. It can also be depressing opposite the recesses and chimney breasts in a 'through' living room; opposite a run of cupboards in a bedroom or at the side of the stairs.

A textured or patterned wall covering may not be the correct answer to the problem, since there may already be several other patterned surfaces in the room. One obvious treatment is to 'pattern with plain' – arrange groups of objects or pictures to produce an impression of a pattern on the surface.

Fix fabric to the wall to cover up an unwanted surface. There are several ways of doing this.

Paper-backed varieties can be stuck on, but may be difficult to remove and tricky to keep clean. For ordinary fabrics, battens can be fixed round the perimeter of the wall and, if necessary, across the wall area. The fabric is then stretched and pinned over the battens, and can be taken down for cleaning. Staple guns are also used for fixing fabric, particularly for a pleated effect. Special fabric tracks are available which are also fixed to the top, bottom and sides of the wall. The fabric is tucked behind the track with a special tool similar to a shoe horn. Fabric may also be hung on a curtain track at the top of the wall with the fabric headed as for curtains – it can then flow free or be pinned at the skirting. Curtain wires at the top and bottom will give a very attractive shirred effect.

FIXING FABRIC TO WALLS

There are several ways of fixing by means of battens pinned round the perimeter with the fabric stretched over them. It can be fixed by a special method called Fabritrak, where metal grooving is fixed to the perimeter and the fabric is slotted into the grooving by means of a special tool rather like a shoe horn. With both these methods the fabric can be removed for cleaning. Fabric can also be stuck to walls (putting the adhesive on the wall, not on the fabric) or stapled. We show this quick and easy method.

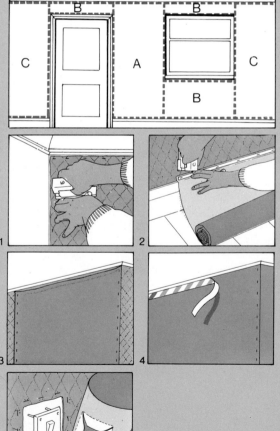

The working order is shown (left). Start in the centre (A) and work outwards, cutting separate pieces of fabric to go above and below doors or windows (B). Finish with the corner sections (C). Staple the underlay straight from the roll (1). Overlap edges slightly when butting together. Leave padding 1cm/$\frac{1}{2}$in clear of the edges of the door. Lay a roll of fabric face down on the floor (2). Turn up 1-2cm/$\frac{1}{2}$-1in fabric, put a strip of card over it and staple along the base through the card. When three sides are fixed, give fabric a good pull upwards to smooth out creases and staple top edge of fabric (3). To hide staples, cover edge of fabric and glue contact tape along the top (4). For fittings, cut a generous hole in the underlay, but the exact size in the fabric (5).

Commission a mural or wall pattern. Alternatively use a photomural or project slides of a changing scene on to the wall area at night.

Add surface interest to a very long, blank wall with panels made from picture-frame beading or quadrant pinned to the wall. Treat the insides of the panels differently from the surrounding wall area – use a different colour, marble, rag-roll or sponge-stipple the surface to create textural contrast, coordinating wall coverings – one inside the panel and the companion outside or mix paper and paint treatments. Wallpaper borders or friezes can be used for a less permanent panelled effect or can be simulated with paint. A border outlining a bedhead or sofa can really highlight the furniture and look very effective. Borders can be bought ready-made or created with stencils. Use paper templates to test the size, shape and positioning of the panels before you make them.

Try the 'dado' treatment on a tall rather than long blank wall area. Divide the wall horizontally, about 1 m/3-3½ ft up, parallel with the skirting, with beading, quadrant or plaster moulding. Treat the lower and upper areas of the wall in different ways. Paper one section and paint the other. Use companion or coordinating papers, such as positive and negative versions of the same design. Hang a heavy, moulded wall covering on the lower half, or fit real or simulated wood panelling. Pin trellis on to either section of the wall, painted to contrast with the background, and set it off in the other section with a floral-and-trellis pattern on paper. This treatment works particularly well in tall halls and long corridors. Paint a trellis or grid pattern to simulate the look of trellis, adding drop shadows to enhance the illusion.

The dramatic drape on door and wall (above right) *is a skilful piece of 'trompe l'oeil' standing out richly against the dark green background. If you don't want a permanent mural, a door can be curtained with real fabric, hung from a special 'portière' rod which rises with the door to permit opening and closing. An exotic eastern atmosphere is created in* this room (right). *The rug, suspended on battens, creates an impression of a tented Turkish interior and softens the angular effect of the beamed ceiling. Rugs can be wall-mounted in many different settings, so long as they are adequately supported. The rattan screening on the shelving adds an interesting texture to this inexpensively furnished room.*

PASSAGES AND HALLWAYS

Large houses and flats may have spacious and well-lit individual rooms, but narrow and gloomy passages and stairwells. To worsen the impression, inner passages are frequently peppered with doorways, often breaking up the wall area in awkward places.

You can create a light and airy effect with the right choice of colour scheme and clever decorations. You may be able to let in some natural daylight, or trap some reflected light, but you may have to face the fact that some form of artificial light will be necessary most of the time.

Solving the problem

Create a terraced effect. Choose the longest, unbroken wall, and decorate with a mural, possibly seen through a colonnade if you like a classical style. Marble all the woodwork to echo the pillars and use trees in pots and indoor plants if there is room and light. If not, paint the plants on the wall to enhance the patio image further. Alternative *trompe l'oeil* effects include a snow scene or seascape, a bright view of spring saplings

or absolutely any scene which you would like to live with.

If the corridor ends in a door, try treating the wall and door at the end in a similar way. Paint a view seen through the door so that it looks as though it is permanently open on to a vista. If there are no artists in the family and you do not want to commission a design, you can create a simpler effect with stylized rolling hills, sky and trees by cutting up self-adhesive plastic in appropriate colours. Scale up a suitable design using squared paper and transfer it on to the door or wall.

Bright, sunshine colours are a simple solution. Paper the walls with a pretty pattern on a light background. Echo the background of the paper for most of the woodwork, but paint all the doors a clear, bright colour. If the paper is multi coloured, you might choose a different hue for each door or paint the ceiling a pale, clear, sky blue.

Create a window on a blank wall using a frame, mirror glass or mirror tiles. Light the area carefully to create a subdued reflected glow.

Dimly lit halls can be brightened up in several ways. Light is provided by fluorescent tubes, concealed behind the coving (1). The light bounces off the ceiling, bringing warmth and a diffused glow to the area. The original door in this hall is given the Gothic treatment (2). A lighting frame is constructed from ceiling panels and used to hide light fittings (3). A fanlight is installed above the door to let in some natural light without losing any privacy (4). Display fittings are built to each side of the front door, and include concealed lighting to illuminate the whole area (5). An inner porch is created from glass bricks, softly diffusing light through the hall (6).

DULL COLOUR SCHEMES

A carefully planned scheme worked around neutral or very pale colours or a monochromatic scheme can look dull and flat. Despite a perfect paint finish it can seem to lack personality. Injecting more life into a dull scheme does not necessarily involve redecorating or refurnishing. First establish why the colours have not worked or what is still missing.

Solving the problem

Create some bright focal points. Often a room looks dull because it lacks accents and accessories or it has insufficient colour contrast. Try a few bright cushions scattered on the sofas and chairs or a colourful handwoven throw-over, a collection of coloured glass in an attractive display, some pretty ornaments, or a well-planned group of pictures and prints, an exotic sculpture or a large piece of unusual pottery. (See page 18 for some colour scheming rules.)

Break up the surface textures if they are too similar or there is not enough balance between patterned and plain surfaces. Add shiny textures to a room with mainly matt finishes, harsh ones to an over-soft scheme and matt surfaces to an over-shiny scheme. Pattern can be added to a plain room without actually providing a patterned surface (see page 30 for guidelines).

Liven up expanses of blank walls which might look dull if they are painted in plain colours in a light-absorbing or uninteresting colour. Try some of the remedies for blank or long walls.

Change the lighting and bring a room to life. Introduce some pools of light from lamps, possibly with lampshades in interesting colours. Try spotlighting some areas or putting concealed lighting behind a pelmet, cornice or coving. Place a decorative rug under a glass table. Don't underestimate the power of houseplants to brighten a room.

Rearrange the furniture – the positioning may add to a dull effect, for example when pieces are squarely placed with backs parallel to the wall. A

sofa can go at right-angles to a wall facing another sofa or two chairs, with a coffee table in between to make an inviting 'conversation area'. In a living/dining room try a similar grouping and back the sofa with a serving table or sideboard, making a natural division between the two parts of the room. In a bedroom move the bedhead away from the wall and suspend fabric from the ceiling to divide the spaces. Alternatively, position wardrobes backing on to the bed, so they open the other way and act as a more solid room divider. That way you will have a separate dressing area, and a cosy, intimate sleeping area. Make a scale plan with cutouts of the furniture shapes (see page 13) to make sure everything will fit in before you move heavy pieces.

Use a cover-up technique. Change the colour of the walls – paint over paper, hang a patterned wall covering or drape them with fabric (see page 128). Break up the overall plainness of large floor areas with one or several rugs. Use pattern on plain and vice versa.

Alter the window dressing. A blind under curtains can add interest if the two contrast with each other, or put up some heavy drapes with flamboyant ties and a pelmet over simple blinds or nets.

SOFT FURNISHINGS

When you move into a new home, your drapes may not fit the existing windows. If they are made from good quality fabric, perhaps lined and interlined, you may not want to change them. It is possible to make curtains 'stretch' to fit, although in some cases it is more sensible to cut them down to fit a smaller window, or to make them into table covers, cushions, lampshades and other accessories.

Existing upholstery can also be a problem in a new environment, especially if you have left your curtains and carpets behind in the old house and either taken on the ones in your new home from the previous occupant or purchased new ones. Again there are several ways of making these soft furnishings fit into your new home.

Solving the problem

Lengthen curtains and drapes. If the headings are simple or pleated with tape, unpick the top and add extra fabric and new heading tape to make them the right length. Cover up the join with a dramatic pelmet or swags and tails at the top of the curtain in a contrasting or complementary fabric.

Trim curtain hems with fringe and braid if the shortfall is not too deep. You can make false hems, or let in bands of contrasting fabric or colour. If you

decide to make a decorative border effect, you can carry it up the sides of the curtains and across a pelmet. Echo the effect in a wallpaper frieze or painted border so it looks like part of the design theme.

Widen narrow curtains in a similar way, with a border trim at each side. If the curtains are pencil or pinch-pleated, change the heading tape for a less tightly-gathered one to gain extra width. If this still does not bridge the gap, buy a contrasting fabric and add wide bands to the outside edges of the curtains. You can contrast patterned with plain fabric, and vice versa. You can also make striped curtains – unpick the seams and let in widths of different fabric – or split widths for a narrower stripe. Again, aim for an integrated look, using the contrasting fabric for a dramatic top treatment to the curtains.

Integrate soft furnishings with new fittings by changing the colour. If the colour is wrong but the curtains fit, you may be able to dye them yourself. Take professional advice before starting. If the fabric is good and the curtains are lined and interlined, have them professionally dyed. You may find that the fabric is not suitable for dyeing for one of several reasons. Some fabrics,

particularly some synthetic fibres, will not dye well. Some fabrics will shrink and, in some cases, the dye can cause the fabric to rot. It is not usually possible to dye from dark to light. Colour can be completely stripped out of some fabrics, but this process badly weakens the fibres – faded curtains may actually shred if colour-stripped. You cannot obliterate pattern with dye, but you do get an interesting textured effect with some designs when you dye them.

Upholstery can sometimes be dyed *in situ* or there are professional firms who will take the furniture away for recolouring. Again, be guided by the experts and do not be surprised if the finished result does not look quite as you expected. It may be better to consider a different approach and use new, loose or tailored covers. As a temporary measure you can make a throw-over cover. Try a lace panel or delicate shawl on a bedroom chair or sofa or use an attractive blanket, rug or piece of patchwork on a leather or tweed cover. You can make a quick throw-over-and-tie cover from inexpensive sheeting bought by the metre/yard, tie-dyed or patterned with batik if it suits the room scheme. Sometimes a vast collection of different-shaped and coloured cushions thrown in profusion on to a sofa or chair will be so striking, that you do not need to recover.

Tented walls provide a perfect cover-up, and add a soft texture to a stark room. The neutral-coloured sitting room (left) has fabric on all four walls, suspended from curtain track mounted at cornice level. The curtains are in the same fabric, so that at night the entire wall area is draped in fabric.

A surrealist stage-set atmosphere (right) in a room designed by fashion designer Zandra Rhodes. Extravagantly tented ceiling, exotic drapes and sumptuous floor cushions are contrasted with the interestingly decorated classic columns. An amazing collection of accessories completes this highly original design.

WOODWORK

It can be surprisingly difficult to decide on a woodwork treatment. It may just not work, but this may not be apparent until the scheme is complete. Yet it is a pity to play safe with neutral-toned doors, skirtings, frames and sills or just to go for the easy option and paint them to match the background wall covering, fabric or carpet.

Painting woodwork white is a mistake if there are off-white items, such as built-in furniture, units or carpets in the scheme. A brilliant white woodwork will make them look dirty unless the walls are also white. If you plan to use a neutral tone, colour-match it to an existing item or background very carefully.

Solving the problem

Create an interesting texture with one of the special painting techniques, such as marbling, rag-rolling, dragging or sponge-stippling. You can brighten or deepen the colour with one of these techniques. Take care to choose the right colour value to put on top of the existing one. Test the effect on a separate piece of paper or card when you are trying one of these attractive texturing methods.

Try stripping all the existing paint from the woodwork down to the natural wood. Clean and then wax or seal the surface. The warm look of polished wood can transform a room scheme. Most available paint strippers allow you to work on a small area at a time. Doors can be difficult to strip, particularly if they have mouldings and panels, and it may be easier to have them 'dipped and stripped' professionally.

Colour stain natural woodwork or stencil a bright pattern on it as an alternative to leaving it stripped. Paint beadings or mouldings on a door in a contrasting colour or a lighter or darker value of the original colour.

The good gloss finish on this door and frame in a contrasting colour to the surrounding wall (left) stands out in relief. This type of door and woodwork often responds well to stripping.

Doors can be taken off their hinges to be worked on or sent away to be professionally stripped. Rag-rolling is a painting technique which gives texture interest to walls and woodwork. The walls are rag-rolled to contrast with the frieze and cornice treatment (above), to add depth, length and height.

KITCHEN AND BATHROOM FITTINGS

When you move into a home with a well-fitted kitchen or bathroom it can be irritating if you do not actually like the colour or style of the units, the finish and design of the worktops, the pattern on the ceramic tiles or the colour of the bathroom sanitary ware. There are ways of giving units and tiles a face-lift that will allow you to modify the design without replacing the fittings.

Solving the problem

Replace unit doors and drawer fronts. Some manufacturers supply spare sections for their cabinets, so find out who made yours and if different colours or designs are available. There are also specialist companies who will make new doors to order. It is only worthwhile changing the doors if the units are of very good quality and the carcasses are strong and sound. Unvarnished wooden cabinet doors of different sizes are also available from large DIY stores.

Cover unit doors and drawer fronts with tongue-and-groove wood cladding for a country look or pin on curved beading for a textural look, first making sure that the additional weight is not too heavy for the existing hinges and frames. Otherwise the doors might warp or drop slightly, making opening and closing difficult.

Set the tongue-and-groove on a diagonal rather than a vertical. Or try a horizontal pattern, which gives a more solid impression than a vertical pattern. Painting the tongue-and-groove in a shiny or satin finish or coloured wood stain will eliminate a rustic look where a contemporary one works best. Alternatively, you can antique the timber and seal it in a matt finish to get a traditional look.

Brighten kitchen units using any of the methods for built-in furniture (see page 123). Note that laminated plastic and melamine-faced surfaces cannot be painted, but can be sprayed with car enamels. All surfaces except for the worktops can be coloured in this way.

If you have cabinets made of wood, try a dragged paintwork look using washable paint in pastel colours. The effects can be quite stunning.

Give units a minor facelift by simply changing handles or knobs and adding a beading trim or a narrow moulding. Bright coloured plastic handles can look extremely good in a modern kitchen.

Siting Fans

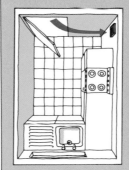

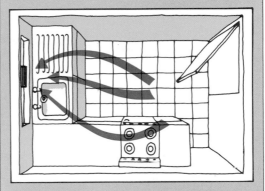

Mount fans in window, wall or ceiling furthest from the air replacement source for maximum air movement. The fan is too close to the door and too far away from cooker and sink (left). The fan is correctly placed in the window above the sink, taking steam and fumes from sink and cooker (below).

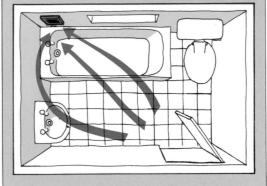

Bathrooms also need good ventilation, particularly if they are internal, windowless areas. The wall-mounted fan simply changes air which comes through the door, and steam is left at the 'action' end of the room (left). The fan is correctly mounted above the tap end of the bath and circulates the air to maximum capacity (below).

Change or cover work surfaces. Some laminates can have a new layer bonded on top. Thick tiles can be used for worktops and can sometimes be applied to an existing surface, but they may need a frame or heavy duty underpinning. Quarry tiles are a good choice. Special worktop tile kits are available, complete with edging tiles and are fairly easy to handle, but should be used with the correct type of tile grouting which is impervious to cooking liquids and acids. Choose a contrasting grout colour for a more striking effect.

Cover up existing wall tiles if you cannot live with the colour or pattern. You can retile on top of old, but if the existing tiles have a heavy 'nosing' (ridge of tiles) round the top, remove this carefully. Neaten the edge with a wood batten after retiling. Alternatively, face the top area of the wall with chipboard, set flush with the existing tiles, and retile the whole wall area.

Tiles can also be covered up with cork in sheet or tile form, but it must be properly sealed. Pre-sealed cork is ideal. Cork is more practical in a bathroom than in a kitchen so long as the atmosphere is not too steamy. Do not use the very granular, crumbly type as it is not strong enough for this purpose.

Hide ugly tiles under a layer of heavy contoured vinyl designed for bathroom and kitchen walls for a temporary disguise – the original grouting may eventually show through. For a more permanent surface, cover tiles with a laminate. It can either be bonded on to the tiles or stuck to a baseboard which is then battened on the wall.

Conceal tiles with wood cladding. There is no need to remove the tiles first. Battens are fixed to the wall and faced with wood cladding using a technique known as 'secret nailing'. If you want to clad a whole wall which is only partly tiled, the battens should be thicker on the area of wall which has no tiles, so the wood cladding will fit flush.

Giving tiles a simple facelift can be achieved with paint, using either special ceramic paint or industrial floor paint. This will not work with heavily textured tiles as the effect may be blotchy. The paint surface will not be particularly durable, so do not expect a long-lasting finish.

Ceramic tiles come in all shapes, sizes, colours and textures (left). Look for interesting border designs and tiles, ridged and marbled textures. Always use a floor grade tile for flooring not a wall grade.

Floor tiles can be made from different materials — cork, carpet, lino, vinyl, marble or thermo-plastic. Make sure you get the right type for the particular job you have in mind. Floor tiles are easy to handle, especially in small, cramped spaces, where intricate cutting is required.

STORAGE SPACE

Adequate storage space is often lacking in modern homes. With a little thought, furnishings can be planned to include either temporary or permanent storage.

Solving the problem

Fix up temporary storage in the bedroom by the simplest possible method. If there are recesses to each side of the chimney breast, put up hooks and rails and a few shelves or pull-out wire racks. You can conceal everything behind blinds. Hang roller blinds or vertical venetians over the alcove and conceal fixings under a pelmet, or use a curtain if you prefer a soft, informal style. If you do not have recessed spaces, buy a dress rail or hire one if it really is to be a temporary arrangement and conceal it behind a screen or floor-to-ceiling curtains.

Use corrugated plastic stacking boxes or bright and cheerful vegetable racks for children's clothes, toys or tools, and store really small items in wire filing trays.

Double-up storage space and a table or work surface. Old cabin trunks, wicker costume or laundry baskets or blanket boxes can be used in this way. For long-term storage, use the container as a bedside table. Castors fixed to the bottom of a heavy trunk or box make it much easier to move.

Use a bentwood hatstand as a decorative bathroom or bedroom stand on which to hang towels and towelling dressing gowns. Traditionally styled clothes horses are also an attractive way of hanging bathroom towels. If you can find an original one, either strip it and apply a polyurethane seal or decorate it with one of the paint techniques such as speckling to match your overall scheme.

Custom-built storage in a narrow kitchen (below left) slopes outwards at the ceiling to give maximum storage, but tapers towards the work surfaces to allow for better light and to avoid the danger of a knock on the head! These bookshelves (below right) fit into a narrow hall neatly and give maximum storage facilities in an awkward area.

RENOVATION AND CAMOUFLAGE

Most properties have one or two drawbacks – no place is ever perfect. They may be the result of a previous owner's mistake or – more depressingly – your own. It could be an actual in-built design fault like an awkwardly shaped room, or one that is too dark or too bright, or a room that is proving impossible to furnish successfully, no matter how many times you change the plan. A room can be too tall, or have a low or sloping ceiling. It can also be too narrow, or box-like, too dark and cold, too bare or too cluttered.

There are some common semi-structural problems, like uneven or rocky floorboards, poor wall surfaces, including bad plasterwork or cracked or crazed tiles, ceilings with missing mouldings or damaged cornices. Woodwork can also take a beating and be in need of a drastic facelift. Doors often need to be replaced or refurbished, staircases can sometimes be badly boxed-in, ugly fireplaces or other fitments and oddly-shaped and placed windows can be an eyesore. Even a wall in the wrong place can ruin your new plan for the room.

However, none of these faults are too difficult to cope with. Most of the design problems can be solved with a clever choice of colour and a deft use of design technique and texture. Any of the semi-structural problems *must* be put right by you or a professional before you undertake any remodelling, refurnishing or redecorating. Beautiful new wall coverings, fabrics and paint will just peel off the wall if you have not left new plaster to dry out for long enough, for example. But modern materials and techniques make it possible to do a great deal to rescue run-down surfaces from the ravages of time.

However, you may find you have more of a major disaster on your hands, especially if you have bought a very run-down old property – possibly damp, dry or wet rot, a leaking roof, plumbing which needs renewing, unsafe electric wiring, woodworm, or 'live' plaster on walls and ceiling (perhaps in danger of falling down). If this is the case you will need to call in the experts to get the necessary help and advice before you do anything.

A qualified architect, surveyor or a good builder should be able to give you an idea of how these faults can be put right and how much they will cost. There are other professionals, like roofing specialists and damp and decay experts, who will also give free advice and estimates for work to be done, so do not hesitate to call on them. If you plan to make any structural alterations of your own, it makes sense to check with a specialist to discover exactly what you can and cannot do. Sometimes you will need agreement for your alterations from the planners in your area, and this all has to be checked before you start work.

Space, too much or too little, can also be a problem. You might have a wonderfully long hall or corridor but a tiny living room. You can, of course, change the shape of the rooms on any floor of a house by knocking down walls and making two rooms into one, or you can rebuild walls elsewhere. This is something which again needs the advice of an architect or surveyor as many internal walls are load-bearing and support either the floor or a wall

Rough wall surfaces can be a problem in old converted properties. Don't be tempted to cover, clad or replaster them. Try to make the wall texture the starting point for the scheme and surface treatments.

Here (above) a converted barn has rough *hewn stone steps leading to the upper floor. The beams are stripped and sealed and the walls are painted to protect and enhance the texture. The iron handrail provides textural contrast and was taken from an outside staircase at the same property.*

in the rooms above. But remodelling the interior of your house in this way can help you make far better use of the available space. Other possibilities include building an extension, redesigning part of the rear of the property to create mezzanine levels linked by short staircases, or converting an attic room. All these ideas could transform your house but professional advice is definitely needed at those critical, planning stages.

RENOVATION

If ceilings, walls, floors, doors, woodwork and windows are showing the ravages of time but are structurally sound, there are ways in which they can be renovated. In some cases a cover-up job is the most practical and the most successful decoratively, but it does rather depend on the actual problem and the type of surface you want to use as part of your basic scheme. It is no good covering a cracked or heavily textured wall surface with wood cladding, for example, if you want to achieve an elegant traditional look as this would be more suited to a modern scheme. But covering the poor surface with draped fabric in a môiré or watered silk will achieve the effect you want.

A poor wall, ceiling or wood surface is often accentuated by its painted surface or wall covering – shiny paints, metallic wall coverings or pale, delicately textured paper will only help to emphasize the problem. A darker colour, a heavier texture for the wall covering, a matt or textured paint or a special painting technique will all help to hide small faults and imperfections. A change of light source can also help. If you have poor walls, try training the main light up on to the ceiling and using diffused pools of lights from lamps. If the ceiling is in poor condition, combine soft background lighting with direct lighting to focus attention on interesting features. If you experiment with some portable fittings, you can plan new lighting positions so that only diffused light falls on the problem area.

The best way to tackle ravaged surfaces is to begin at the top and work down.

This warehouse conversion (above left and right) enhances many of the original features. The wood clad ceiling is retained and refurbished, with the metal tie bars and roof trusses picked out to contrast with and emphasize the roof shape.

The brickwork has been exposed, cleaned and left natural on part of the wall area to provide textural interest. Part is smooth plastered and serves as a foil, throwing the brick into relief. The gallery, built of stone and wood, again adds textural contrast, which is in keeping with the rest of the structure. Metal handrails are coloured to match the ceiling framing.

Start with the ceiling

Really bad plasterwork must be taken down because there is a very real danger of it falling down – seek expert advice and call in a plasterer to check it if you are not too sure. The ceiling can be replastered or replaced with plasterboard and painted or wallpapered to suit your colour scheme. Avoid the temptation, however, of painting a rippled or heavily textured surface in place of the old. This is very difficult to remove. It may actually be one of your present problems. Covering up a poor ceiling with ceiling or acoustic tiles is another way of botching the job and again these can be very difficult to remove if you want a change of style.

If you have a ceiling that is not too bad structurally but has a decorative surface that is just not to your taste, you may be able to camouflage it quite successfully. A smooth but slightly cracked or bumpy ceiling can be covered with a special vinyl ceiling paper that has a fine linen-like texture and a fabric backing (this is not too difficult to remove if you want a change later) and then painted – a darker colour and matt paint will help to disguise faults. If the ceiling is low, do not use too dark a colour as this will just emphasize the lack of height. A boldly patterned paper is again a good cover for uneven ceilings. Use one with a flowing, non-directional pattern rather than one with a geometric design which can be difficult to hang. A cleverly painted pattern can also help, particularly if there is only one bad area. Hang some patterned or plain fabric ceiling banners or hangings looped over fixed poles or wires. Alternatively, make a big decorative kite and conceal some lights above it. Wood cladding, particularly in the form of tongue-and-grooved boards, blends equally well in both modern and traditional settings. Try running the boards diagonally where a very contemporary effect is required. Wood laminated panels should be selected with care because they can look somewhat insensitive. Both methods will effectively cover a multitude of sins and can be removed if you decide on another treatment later on. Another method is to run boards across the ceiling on lowered battens leaving spaces in between. The hidden ceiling can be painted in a darker colour with lighting fixed above the boards or spotlights can be clipped on as required. Bear in mind, however, that cladded ceilings can make a room seem claustrophobic, particularly if the ceiling is already too low unless it is stained in a very light wood stain or painted a light colour.

Older properties may already have a fantastic ceiling which only needs renovating, restoring or refurbishing.

In the modern extension to an old cottage (right), *the gap between modern and traditional styles is bridged by a beamed ceiling, which echoes the dark old beams of the original building and the wooden floor laid throughout.*

The tented ceiling lends an exotic feel to this dining area (below).

Tenting with fabric is another good way of covering up an ugly ceiling – it can look wonderfully romantic in a bedroom and sumptuously elegant in a dining room. You can also add a layer of insulation behind the fabric to help keep the room warm. Many of the companies who will hang fabric for you suggest this (and tenting walls) and a special material is produced for the purpose.

If you have an older property there may be a dent in the ceiling where a moulding is missing or damage to part of the decorative plasterwork on the ceiling, cornice or coving. Treatment will depend on the extent of the damage – if it is very slight you may be able to repair it with a little *trompe l'oeil* by painting in the missing piece. Or applying some filler might well be the answer. If the problem is more extensive, there are several ways of solving it. Many manufacturers make fibrous plaster copies of ceiling roses, mouldings and cornices, so you may be able to get a replacement which is virtually

identical. It may mean replacing a run of moulding or coving if the join is not to be too obvious. If your ceiling is more ornate and the pattern is one which is not popular enough to be copied, then there are specialist plasterers who will make up matching pieces to order – but look in the catalogues first.

Decorative ceilings are a marvellous architectural feature, and if you have one, treat it with respect and restore it with care. If you colour the 'bed' (the flat part) and pick out the plasterwork in white or a light colour to contrast, the effect will be even more dramatic.

You may not realize that you have beautifully decorated plasterwork above your head if the property is old and the details have become clogged up with layers of paint over the years. Cornices may just look rigid or bumpy and poorly textured. It is well worth the time and effort to remove the residue of paint, restoring any parts where necessary and then making sure any new paint does not fill up the indentations again. Many modern, water-based paints are suitable for ceilings, but do not use a shiny oil-based paint as it can be too reflective.

Timber beams, which are exposed in some older country and cottage-type properties, may also need restoring. If the problem is one of decay or woodworm, call in the relevant expert. New pieces of timber can be spliced in with an invisible join. In the past it was fashionable to use heavy stains or even creosote on wooden beams to preserve them. The stain can be removed and the beams then bleached or sand-blasted.

If you want to make a beamed ceiling seem taller but major building work is out of the question, you could consider painting the beams a light colour or white to match the plaster between. Many traditionalists would be horrified at this idea but it is all a question of personal taste and dark beams bearing down on your head can be uncomfortable to live with. The beams will appear less obvious if the plaster between them is painted in a rich colour of the same tonal value as the wood.

Carry on with the walls

Some of the problems with walls are the same as with ceilings. They often suffer from old bumpy or 'live' plaster. But again, if the surface is in a really bad condition, call on expert help and advice.

Quite a few of the cover-up techniques already suggested for ceilings will work well with walls, but if you want a plain painted surface or a beautiful, delicately textured wall covering, you must have a really good surface as a starting point. This may involve replastering some areas or covering them with plasterboard, insulation board or chipboard before decorating.

Again, remember that foil and metallic wall coverings, light colours, shiny and delicate textures (paint or wall coverings) will just highlight any imperfections. You may find you have to change your mind and use a different treatment from the one you first thought of and use a strongly-patterned paper, for example, instead of a plain surface. Again you can try altering the lighting (as suggested for ceilings), and if direct sun and daylight shines strongly on the wall, filter it through net or voile drapes, gauze blinds or adjustable venetian blinds.

Most of the painting techniques such as marbling, dragging, rag-rolling or sponge-stippling work extremely well and are a good disguise for a fairly bumpy wall surface. A fairly heavily textured wall covering of the type intended for over-painting is also an effective camouflage for poor plaster. But remember, this can be difficult to remove once it has been over-painted several times, and if you inherit this type of wall treatment or the really heavy type of relief wall covering painted with gloss paint, you will probably need to hire a steam-stripping machine to remove it – a process which may then damage the plaster underneath. The same comments apply if the plaster itself has been roughened up, or a textured paint has been applied – softening the paint and removing it is almost impossible. The only solution if you want to repaint is to sand down the existing textured

Roughcast plasterwork in a cottage bedroom (above) blends well with the wood textures and white linen bedcover. The only pattern is added in the rug. This country-style kitchen in a farmhouse has an original slate floor (right). The walls are roughly plastered, but painted for practical purposes, and a tiled splash back protects the essential wall area.

surface with an electric sander.

Wood cladding, insulation or plasterboard can be battened on to walls and will cover up most bad or ugly surfaces so long as the battens can be firmly fixed. Laminated panels can be fixed in a similar way, although they can also be glued. Cork cladding, which is usually glued to a wall, can also be mounted on a base (like chipboard) before battening on. This is a practical idea if you think you are likely to want a change in a few years' time. Mirrors or mirror tiles can be mounted in the same way before fixing them to a very uneven surface.

Plaster can always be hacked off and the original brick wall exposed. But do make sure before you start work that the wall is brick and not just a partition wall of breeze block, plasterboard or timber. The brick should then be cleaned and sealed. Walls can also be resurfaced using stone,

brick or slate (see surface treatments, page 16) if this suits the type of house, style of decorating and furnishing you intend.

If you already have wood cladding or panelling but it is too dark, stained an unpleasant colour or painted, try to strip it back to the bare wood and then seal or wax it. Or if natural wood just does not fit in with your design scheme, you can paint it. However, if you have a very old house with genuine panelling, think very carefully before you do anything so drastic.

Occasionally what looks like fine old panelling is actually 1920s or 30s imitation called scumbling, where inferior wood is stained and glazed to simulate a particular wood grain and colour, and you only discover this after you have spent hours stripping it. If in doubt, call in the experts for an opinion before you start work.

Crazed or discoloured tiles can be another unsightly problem. You can retile on top of tiles, but not if they are cracked or broken (see page 136). Any of the methods of covering up poor plaster can also be used for a tiled wall so long as the treatment is appropriate. Alternatively, use one of the quick and easy cover-ups suggested on page 136.

Wood, stone and brick all combine to give this Safari-style sitting room (left) an authentic feel. A feature is made out of a necessity (above) — the fire hood and chimney become a focal point in this sitting room, filled with plant and cane furniture which give a conservatory feel to the dining area. The exposed brick and metal and rattan hanging all add textural interest.

Get down to the floor

The floor may not really be a problem area – you may simply have difficulty in deciding what type of treatment to use on it and what floor covering to select. If you do not know what type of flooring you have, look it up on the flooring chart (see page 178) or in the run down of flooring types (see page 15). If the existing surface seems damaged, uneven or damp, call in an expert flooring contractor to see what can be done.

A solid floor which is uneven, cracked or pitted can usually be treated fairly easily with a self-smoothing and self-levelling compound. The floor can then be treated as new and any suitable floor covering or permanent or semi-permanent flooring placed on it.

If floorboards are loose, creaking or uneven because they have been lifted to lay cables, central heating and plumbing pipes, they can usually be screwed or nailed down to the joists beneath to secure them. Check on the pipe and cable runs before you start work. Gaps between boards which have shrunk can be filled with thin strips of wood or filled with *papier mâché*. Very small gaps can be filled with wood filler.

Uneven floorboards need to be level. If they are not, the edge of the boards could work through any floor covering, causing it to split, crack or fray. The easiest way is to fix the boards down firmly and then cover them with hardboard (rough side uppermost if you want a good grip for a new floor covering) or flooring grade chipboard, screwed into

The herringbone effect flooring (top right) *is sheet vinyl, but could be laid in tile, wood, brick, special pavers or even carpet tiles cut to a slim shape. The look is timeless and blends happily with almost any type of scheme, furniture and furnishings.*

A linen drugget has been used on the floor of a simply furnished bedsitting room (centre right), which relies heavily on textural contrast to provide interest. The screened light filtering through into the room adds an extra dimension to the scheme.

A simply patterned, fringed rug softens the sitting area in a large living room (bottom right). *The highly polished wood floor is ideal in a room which doubles as a gallery. In large, long rooms, a change of floor can help zone the areas and make the room appear less long.*

Again, a simply patterned
Oriental rug on polished
floorboards creates a
dramatic effect (below),
but this time the rug is
painted not real.

Exposed floorboards laid
diagonally (below right).
The rich blue stain
contrasts with the pink
and white bedroom
scheme. Stained
floorboards are best
protected with several
coats of clear anti-slip
polyurethane varnish.

position. If you plan to lay a ceramic tiled or other
heavy floor upstairs, you must again check on the
strength of the joists to see whether they will take
the weight and make sure there is no movement in
the floor as this will cause the tiles to crack or
break. It may also be necessary to lay a
floor-levelling compound or other subfloor. Again,
if you are at all unsure, seek the advice of an expert.

If the floorboards are sound but are painted or
badly stained, one cunning solution is to have
them taken up and laid back the other way round.
There may be some marking where they crossed
the joists, but this should not be too difficult to
remove by sanding. Sound boards can be stripped
and sanded and are then ready for the decorative
treatment of your choice. This can include
painting, staining and sealing, stencilling or even
marbling.

If your floor is carpeted and the carpet is of good
quality and in good condition, avoid the
temptation of laying new carpet on top of old. Even
laying new carpet on top of old underlay is a
mistake, since the wear pattern transfers itself
quickly to the new carpet.

Openings, staircases and woodwork
The flesh on the bones of a room – the door and
windows, door handles, locks and catches, internal
shutters, stairs and handrail, fireplaces, fitments
and other built-in fittings, all need to be
architecturally right for your choice of interior
design and the style of the property.

Decorative doors leading from a hallway into a sitting area (left) incorporate some original stained glass. Doors can be adapted to let in light this way by removing panels or part of the door, and installing stained or obscured glass to maintain privacy.

A clever idea (below) uses a screen door faced in a single sheet of mirror, providing reflected light and increasing the apparent size of the room.

Doors The wrong door, for example, can completely spoil a cottage-style room where the traditional doors were generally made of planked timber with heavy latch and hinges. A flush-panelled door would just not look right in a scheme for a much older house. The ubiquitous louvred door, looks right in a modern setting and tambour-type and metal louvres fit into a room with High tech furnishings. In some older properties, the original doors may simply have been covered up to give an easy-to-decorate surface, so take the doors off their hinges and investigate.

When doors are used as dividers – between two areas of a large room or between two inter-communicating rooms – it is even more important that they are seen as an integral part of the decorating scheme. If they are unattractive, think about changing them for doors that will fit into your scheme or decorate them so they merge into the background. Decorated doors can also brighten up dull areas like long corridors. They can also be included in a fantasy painting in a child's or teenager's room, or as part of a *trompe l'oeil* in another setting.

Attractive doors which are in good condition can be stripped back to the natural wood and sealed to enhance a scheme. Plain doors can be decorated to look panelled or beading can be added to simulate panelling. Many of the paint techniques are particularly suitable for doors. They can be decorated boldly so that they stand out from the background and become a focal point or treated in such a way that they blend into it.

Staircases need to be sound – if you have problems with creaks and groans, wobbly treads or shaky bannisters, get a carpenter or builder to check them out and carry out the necessary replacement or

This sweeping staircase (below) is a modified version of the original — new balustrading gives a 1930s Cunard look to this open-plan beachhouse. The sitting out area under the staircase is provided by a softly sculptured settee which echoes the line of the stair treads.

A space-saving spiral staircase (right) gives a light, airy look to this maisonette. The curved wall structure links with the bookshelf construction providing firm support with visual lightness.

repairs. Damaged balusters can be removed and new ones installed. Copies of many different styles are readily available from timber yards and wood merchants. Shaky handrails and bannisters can be removed and a new unit made in wrought iron installed. This can also be effective with solid staircases where wrought iron can be fitted in a style to suit the hall and stair area.

In some older properties, lovely handrails, newel posts and balusters may have been boxed-in to make decorating easier. These are well worth uncovering and repairing if necessary. Or if the boxing-in is sleek and attractive, paint it using one of the special painting techniques – marbling works well here. Another alternative is to simulate stone balusters in paint.

If the hall and landing area is cramped or dark, replacing the stairs may well be the best way of solving the problem. Adapt your existing staircase

or put in an open-tread staircase, for example, to let in a lot of extra light. A spiral staircase will save a lot of space as well as looking decorative. When a complete conversion is being considered, a staircase can be moved to allow for more space. It could become an integral part of the living area, leaving the old hall and landing area for other purposes. Alternatively, the stair, hall or landing area of a small house may become part of one open-plan living room. It is important to choose the stairway design, treads, bannisters or balusters and handrail very carefully, as they actually become part of the room design. It can become the main focal point or be seen as a large piece of statuary and be highlighted with uplighters. Altering the position of a staircase or installing a new one is a major undertaking and again you will need to call in a qualified architect, surveyor or a good builder, to help you with your plan.

Windows and their treatment are discussed in detail on pages 103 to 113, but no amount of clever dressing will disguise a window which is just not right for a room. Again it is very much a question of style – the type of window should suit the architecture of the room and the way in which it has been furnished and decorated. In many houses the original windows have been taken out and new ones fitted, which can be totally unsuitable for the existing style. Sometimes properties are given over ornate lattice-type windows, bull's eye panes or quaint bow-fronted and bay windows when the style of the house is very simple. If possible, restore any existing windows or replace them with the appropriate style. Again you may have to seek the advice of an architect to help solve the problem. Think about windows in relation to the façade of the house as well as the effect from inside the room.

Different shaped windows all featured on one wall or a window which is cramped up in one corner can be replaced on the window openings made larger or smaller, or the position altered. There are ways, however, of making visual improvements from the inside of the house which do not involve any major structural change (see pages 103 to 113). Care should be taken when changing windows to ensure that the effect is also good from outside, and does not quarrel with the original architecture. A sliding, patio-style window can do a lot to improve a dark downstairs room, creating a wall of glass which is not so much a window as a see-through wall and can blend in with many different types of building. Windows or doors which lead out to a conservatory or on to a terrace in an older property, however, should be in keeping with the existing interior and exterior architectural styles.

Two windows (left and above) *with their own distinctive design style. Both add character, and are in keeping with the architectural look of the room. The circular one is an inspired treatment for a double door and the five-sided attic window follows the roof shape.*

Two treatments for a room-with-no-view (top right). *A wall of glass bricks lets in maximum light and incorporates a small window for ventilation. The Gothic-paned window is a decorative item in its own right, and the interesting shape stands out against the plain red wall.*

The magnificent view becomes a mural along one side of a sitting room/kitchen area in a holiday home (centre right). The huge-paned windows help to echo the cruise ship atmosphere and draw attention away from some of the structural pipework.

Intriguing lozenge-shaped window (right) adds decorative interest to a plain wall, and is shuttered for privacy and safety at night. Again the window can be enjoyed for its own sake and for the view which looks like a framed print.

CAMOUFLAGE

Tall rooms

If you have a room which just seems too tall try emphasizing the horizontal lines to take the eye away from the vertical ones – pick out a picture rail and frieze above it in a colour contrasting with the rest of the wall area and ceiling, cornice or coving. Highlight a dado rail in the same colour as the skirting and any other horizontal trims. Contrast the two walled areas above and below the rail, using paint on one half and paper on the other. Alternatively, you can paint the areas in complementary colours, or use two coordinated wall coverings.

In a modern style room, try a patterned wall covering with a horizontal design, or perhaps hang a striped wallpaper horizontally across the room instead of vertically – the stripes need not be contrasting in colour but can be quite subtle. Wall-to-wall curtains with a definite border or horizontal design can also be effective. Try strongly coloured floor coverings and furniture to keep the eye-level down.

Too tall rooms can also be ideal for a split-level furniture design which in turn helps to reduce the apparent height. In a multi-purpose room, a bed can be built on to a raised platform with storage below, or above a desk. Similarly, a dining room could be separated from the living area by a change of level. Hanging pendant lights quite low at regular intervals or a cluster at different heights can also be effective with very high ceilings.

Light the room inventively to draw attention to pools of light which focus on well-planned features in the room such as a special collection of sculpture or glass. Always keep the ceiling in shadow or light with diffused lighting hidden behind a horizontal pelmet.

Try any of these remedies before you do anything as drastic as putting in any form of false ceiling. Lowering the ceiling is not very effective and can spoil the proportions of the room.

Long and narrow rooms

If you feel you are being oppressed in a long, narrow room try just re-arranging the furniture. If you do not want to have to move heavy sofas or chairs around the room you can work out what will fit where by making a scale plan (see page 12). Try placing large pieces of furniture, like a sofa, a table, or a run of unit, at right-angles to a long wall so that they form a natural division. This will make the

The split-level galleried living area (left) *really is tall, but the strong horizontal lines, which are part of the structure. help to counter-balance this.*

The rich colour of the natural wood stands out against the white painted walls, and the heavily beamed and wood clad ceiling helps lower the height visually. A ceiling like this would be too oppressive in a smaller, lower room.

The dark ceiling, cornice and frieze make this sitting room seem smaller and lower (left) *as they*

contrast sharply with the bright red walls. The floor is also in a similar dark tone to the ceiling and adds to the illusion of a lower room. The large mirror in the recess gives reflected light and helps lighten the richness of the scheme.

The long, narrow room (above) *is little more than a corridor! The furniture helps redress the balance, with strongly coloured upholstery and contrasting slab topped table, and the bold horizontal lines of the shelving and window.*

room seem shorter while allowing you to create an open space again when it is needed for entertaining or a special party. Kitchens which are too long can be divided with fitted units and worktops.

You can 'zone' areas of a multi-purpose room in this way. If it is a bedroom, you can create a dressing area by dividing off part of the room with wardrobes, bedroom units and chests of drawers placed to face inwards towards the dressing area. Back them with fabric or some type of wall covering or other decorative surface – this might then form the bedhead wall. Any gaps to the side of the wardrobes or above the chest could be closed with vertical, venetian, roller or festooned blinds in colours to suit the scheme of the room. This treatment can also work well in a room which may have to be shared.

Another way of dividing up areas depends on the type of floor treatments used. You can treat the floor of the dining area or dressing area differently from the sitting or sleeping area, for example. Make it practical and washable in one area, perhaps using vinyl or cork tiles, and softer, more relaxing underfoot in the other, by laying a long pile carpet. If the floor is carpeted throughout you can put a boldly designed or contrasting rug on top and group furniture round it to form a 'conversation' area.

You can help to bring the ends of the room closer together if you decorate them in a darker or stronger colour, use a boldly patterned paper or try wall-to-wall curtains. You can also create a striped effect across the wall and window with a border in paint or a paper fringe on the wall, and a fabric border on the curtains.

Another way to improve the room is to emphasize one of the long walls. In a bedroom it could be used for a wide run of wardrobes, perhaps with mirror-fronted doors magnifying the apparent size and width of the room. If the wall is without recesses or projections, try making some niches, or use wall-mounted shelves and unit furniture.

If you feel the room would look better with some kind of divider, use pale-coloured screens, vertical blinds, drapes or glazed or solid folding doors.

Make an interesting feature of the floor by having stripes go *across* the room widthways. This can be done by painting or staining floorboards, laying carpet with a bold directional pattern across the room or using two-tone tiles to create wide stripes. Border or inlay techniques can be used to outline specific areas.

Low rooms

If your room is too squat or the ceiling slopes creating unusual angles, keep the room simple and furnish it with floor cushions, divan beds or low-slung seating. Create a conversation area or sleeping pit. Buy small, neat pieces of furniture for a period setting.

Paint the ceiling a pale, cool colour and the walls just a shade or two darker. Try giving the ceiling the vista treatment – decorate it to look like the sky seen through openings in billowing clouds, or pale stars on a very soft blue ground. If there are mouldings, cornices or beams, see the suggestions on page 15.

When a ceiling slopes it can be decorated with a mini-print pattern which diffuses the angles. Carry the pattern on to the walls and coordinate it with the window treatment. So long as the colours are pale and the pattern self-effacing, the overall effect will not be overpowering. Coping with a slope can provoke creative design solutions, for example trimming the edges of an angular slope with a border paper or stencilled design.

Throw as much light as possible on to the ceiling – use uplighters and paint the ceiling with a shiny or satin surface or possibly use a reflective paper for a striking effect.

Tiny rooms

Some modern houses, country cottages and apartments often have one or two very small rooms. Solve this design fault according to the function of the room. In some cases, emphasizing the small, cosy atmosphere may be the answer. Treat a small dining room to look even more intimate using rich, dark warm colours and soft textures but keeping patterns muted. Give a small bedroom an exotic look with a tented ceiling and fabric-draped walls in rich, warm colours. Make a study inviting with thick-pile carpets, subdued lighting (except for the desk lamp) and an expensive textured wall treatment such as suede or suede-like fabric.

If your tiny room is the lavatory, you may be able to indulge your sense of the ridiculous, and decorate it with some interesting *trompe l'oeil*, try the inside of a padded cell, for example, or paint a really interesting mural. You could fit small bookshelves or you could just use it as a collector's corner tiling it with a patchwork of different tiles. Making a collage from postcards and pictures can be easy to do, but extremely striking.

This small bathroom in a timber-framed cottage (above) has sloping ceilings and is literally triangular in shape. The cross beaming has a strong horizontal feel to it, and contrasts nicely in texture and colour with the white plastered walls. Combined with the clever building-in of bath and basin, this adjusts the proportions visually.

In the second bathroom (above right) the strong trellis pattern on the walls

and ceiling is bold enough to bring the walls in, and the coloured cornice and patterned ceiling help lower the apparent height.

The L-shaped bedroom (below right) is divided by a blind to separate the sleeping area from the dressing and study area. The room relies on reflected light from mirrors to prevent the narrow end from being too dark.

Keep furniture for small rooms neat and compact and use a mirror or mirror tiles to face cupboard and wardrobe doors to double the apparent size of the room. A few well-chosen pieces of large furniture can make a small room appear to be larger. Breaking the room up with too many small pieces can have the opposite effect. Make any built-in furniture and units merge with the background by painting them all the same colour or to match the background of the wall covering. Some of the more subdued painted surface techniques particularly come into their own here, so long as they are done in pastel colours – try rag-rolling or sponge-stippling.

For small bathrooms, the cosy look can be translated into warm wood cladding on ceilings and walls. Try to expand the size of the room with light, shiny wall and ceiling treatments. Remember

shiny surfaces reflect light and make an area look larger, but they do also show up any surface imperfections. In a bathroom, ceramic or mirror tiles, or mirrors can be used very effectively to make the room seem larger. Light-coloured glossy paint and foil wall coverings also look good. Cleverly designed shelving fitted around a cramped wash basin can be extremely useful for extra storage. You can increase the apparent size of the floor by taking the flooring up on to the bath panel or again use mirrors or mirror tiles. This flooring trick can be used in other small rooms, by painting the skirting to match the floor or laying light and dark coloured tiles alternately, to form a chequerboard pattern which will make the floor look larger – or 'stretch' the room by laying tiles diamond-fashion, from corner to corner.

A striped floor laid diagonally will visually increase the size of a room. Use floor boards, cork tiles or a carpet with a diagonal design.

Basically with small rooms, you should always keep the size of any pattern scaled-down to suit the surface on which it is used, and choose pale, cool colours. Monochromatic colour schemes will help to make a small room look larger (see page 21).

L-shaped rooms

Some rooms are long and narrow with a square fitted to the end – the traditional L-shaped room. These rooms are often spacious and elegant but can be difficult to furnish satisfactorily. Avoid the temptation to clutter them up with dividers, unless you need to cut off a corner for a particular reason, such as a quiet study or hobby area.

You can use some of the furniture arranging suggestions for long narrow rooms in an L-shaped room. The colour scheme should be planned as for one room to unify the two sections, although you can employ some of the foreshortening tricks to make it appear less long.

In some L-shaped rooms, the end of the 'L' is too dark, and it is not always possible to install a window to let in natural light. Reflected light can be used here, either with mirrors or by glazing or part-glazing doors. Sometimes the narrow end of the 'L' is an ideal place to build or position a wall of shelves and units, which could then be lit by concealed lighting from above, and bounced off mirrors on the wall at the back. It could also be the ideal position to feature a large, favourite picture, wall hanging or piece of designer furniture and have it highlighted with a spotlight.

Strangely shaped windows can become the focal point of a room. The circular, highly-placed window (right) has had steps made up to it, and a window seat incorporated into the scheme, so that the sun and unspoilt view can be enjoyed to the full. In the attic playroom (centre), the window frames help to make the room appear wider and the wall less triangular. They are also practical for ventilation. The window frame can be used as a display and toy shelf, and again the country view can be appreciated and become a backdrop to imaginative games.

Subtle, diffused lighting thrown up on to the ceiling by uplighters can help with the balance of this type of room. The rest of the lighting for the room can come from strategically placed lamps and spotlights.

Try dividing the areas by contrasting floorings, as with long rooms, or lay patterned flooring across the width if you need to play the widening trick. You can even break up the floor area visually by laying flooring widthways across the long part of the room, and changing direction at the apex of the L-shape.

If an L-shaped room is fairly tall, a raised platform, with a railed gallery can make an interesting visual break, and create plenty of storage space under the platform. This area can then be used for dining, sitting, listening to music or watching television. If there is sufficient light, a really effective and dramatic treatment is to make the end of the room into an indoor conservatory, divided from the rest of the room with a tracery of arches or trellis, and filled with shrubs, trees and plants, lit by spotlights and uplighters.

If an L-shaped room is being used as a bedroom, the extra section could be the ideal place for a dressing room or bathroom. Attractive screens can be used to sub-divide the area or alternatively fitted cupboards can be built across it.

Strange-shaped windows

One semi-structural problem can be awkwardly placed windows or several different-sized or shaped windows in one wall. To alter the structure of the windows may not be worthwhile, and changes may not work externally.

Window problems, different sizes, shapes and treatments are covered in Windows (see pages 103 to 113). Try not to cover up a window with an interesting shape. All too often one of the irregularly-shaped windows is beautifully proportioned and looks right in the room, while the others are ugly and perhaps too high or too low. The secret is to try and create a sense of unity. This can be done by covering the entire window wall with venetian blinds, floor-to-ceiling nets or lace curtains combined with heavy over-drapes. Another possible treatment is to have important, but false curtains to each side of the window wall, with a pelmet or attractive pole above. Companion or contrasting roller, venetian, festoon or roman blinds can be fitted to each window if appropriate. The most attractive window could be highlighted by painting the frame to contrast with the surrounding wall area, with the frames of the others painted to blend with the wall decoration. Blinds to match the wall treatment, or perhaps painted with a false view could be permanently

A fireplace can become a focal point, and add interest to a small, box-like room. It can make a long, narrow room seem wider or draw attention away from an ugly structure. But the fireplace may not be needed for warmth. Here (left) an old pine fireplace with heavy overmantle has been stripped, sanded smooth and sealed with matt polyurethane varnish. The actual fireplace was removed and a wine rack built in to the gap. Such fireplace openings can often be used for storage, or to display plants, well lit statuary or other special treasures. Fireplace openings can also be filled with wood or multi-fuel stoves, which look decorative in their own right.

closed if there is enough daylight.

Some windows are so high up that they serve no purpose other than letting in a little extra light, or they may be circular in shape and be impossible to curtain. A collection of coloured glass can be displayed which will throw attractive, coloured shadows on to floor or walls when the sun shines. A stained glass panel, decoratively interesting in itself, is another possible solution.

If the window is small, perhaps in a recess, and lets in little light, it might make more sense to convert it into an alcove. Remove the catches and handles, fill in the back flush with plywood or chipboard, and suspend shelves across the opening, choosing these to contrast with the background colour on the wall, and illuminate by concealed lighting from above. If the area is a bit dark, the back of the recess can be covered with mirror glass.

Box-shaped rooms

Many rooms are neither too high, too low, too long or too narrow – they are simply lacking in character. You can have a lot of fun adding atmosphere and style to rooms like this. Once again, the function of the room will influence your choice to some extent – and so will the basic style you want to create taking into account the overall style of the house or apartment.

First of all try to create a focal point in the room – this could be a fireplace or a large piece of furniture in a living room, the bedhead or an interesting piece of furniture in the bedroom or a window treatment in almost any room. In the right situation, a mural or decorative wall treatment can open up a square room completely. If you prefer a changing scene, group pictures or prints together, and move them round from time to time to give a different emphasis.

Interesting ceiling treatments will help alter the proportion of a room that is too square – cladding with wood, tiles or fabric, or paper or paint with an interesting pattern or design. Tented fabric ceilings look exotic in the right setting, such as a bedroom or cosy sitting room.

Making a feature of one wall is another good way of improving a characterless room. Wood, cork, slate, brick or stone cladding will all work well where appropriate. Use a wall of furniture or feature books on display shelves in living areas and feature units or wardrobes with unusual door treatments in the bedroom. In the bathroom or kitchen try tiling one wall only – or do three walls plain and one with a special ceramic tiled panel. Emphasize windows on one wall by making dramatic floor-to-ceiling and wall-to-wall curtains, even if there is only one, medium-sized window – or try this effect with vertical blinds.

A clever floor treatment can also be used to improve a boring room. Try using a definite bold pattern diagonally across the room from corner to corner, either by cutting and fitting floor tiles or painting, staining or laying floor boards or solid floors. Carpet in a decorative way, or use vinyl or linoleum sheet flooring to form inlaid patterns. Outline features of a room – a group of furniture, bed, bath, or a run of units – with border design using tiles or sheet material in kitchens and bathrooms and carpet in living areas.

Triangular-shaped rooms

Some rooms are such strange shapes that they seem almost triangular. If you have a room which is horizontally triangular, try to disguise it by using pale colours and simple patterns on the two walls which seem to form the 'point' and treat the other wall more boldly in a strong colour of paint or with a distinctly patterned wall covering. Alternatively, you can treat all three walls in a different way. Avoid fitting furniture into this type of room if possible, since this can emphasize the narrow end but use wall-mounted corner cupboards, for example, to flatten out the corner. Arrange furniture in such a way that it creates the same effect. If you have a talent for painting or know an artist, you can paint a scene across the apex to flatten it out. Avoid patterns with straight lines and regular repeats in this style of room. The floor can have a fairly bold pattern on it, but consider a floral or indefinite design for the other surfaces.

If you live in a large, old house, the hall and stairwell may be an area for visual improvement – the atmosphere may be cold and unwelcoming as well as being vertically triangular. First of all, use a warm, bold colour scheme, and try to emphasize the base of the triangle by an interesting treatment

for the lower wall level and by selecting an unusual floor covering Graduate the colour of the wall above from dark to light, to minimize the apex effect. This can be done by painting the whole wall a mid-tone, and then stippling, rag-rolling or sponging with a darker and lighter colour to make it lighter at the top, and darker at the bottom.

Projections and recesses

If you have a room which has many projections and recesses there are two ways of treating them: either emphasize and make a design feature out of them or decorate to detract from them.

If you want to emphasize recesses, make them into proper alcoves, where appropriate with arched tops, built-in shelves and concealed lighting or make full use of them for decorative pieces of furniture. Treat the backs and sides of these alcoves differently from the surrounding wall area. If you want to detract from them, fill them with furniture, and decorate the alcove, the furniture, and the surrounding wall area with the same colour, texture or paint finish.

If the recesses are caused by a chimney breast projecting into the room, it may be possible to flatten the wall. This is a structural job, however, and you will need to seek professional advice. If this is not feasible then make a focal point of the fireplace, and carry the treatment round into the recesses. For example, echo the line of the top of the surround with a shelf or built-in cupboards in the recess. Or stone-clad or brick-clad the fireplace to a suitable height, finish with a shelf, and take the shelf or cladding round into the recess.

Take the emphasis away from the problem wall, by highlighting the other walls. If a projection is part of a wall forming an arch between two rooms, you can emphasize it by painting or papering it a different colour from the walls at right-angles or outline the arch with a border or stencil pattern.

Rooms need not be triangular, but they can have a definite tapered feel, like this sitting room (left) *with bold corner windows and the fireplace at the apex. Once 'cornered' in this way, emphasizing the effect is often the best solution to the problem.*

The triangular area under the stairs (below) *is often so much wasted space — in this house it is used as a wine store with triangular custom-built racks. The long corridor* (right) *has sloping ceilings offset by very bold window frames, which exaggerate the character and charm.*

SECTION FOUR

A SENSE OF STYLE

There are many different types of decoration which will give a room a specific style or atmosphere, from the classical and traditional look found in many country houses and stately homes to the modern minimal mood seen in homes throughout Europe, North America and Australia.

Style can be created by a combination of the type of pattern which is used on the various surfaces of the room and the colours and textures which are selected. These are then imposed on the basic room, making allowances for its size, shape and good and bad features (see pages 15-17). Start by detailing all of these. Look at the room and decide what to keep and enhance, and what to remove or disguise. You will then need to cope with the basic shell, selecting suitable patterns, textures and colours for the floors, walls, ceiling and woodwork and choosing suitable window treatments (see page 98). Then consider the major buys – furniture, storage, appliances and equipment. Finishing touches in the form of accents, lighting and accessories will add the final gloss to the scheme. A selection of styles is delineated here to help you identify your likes and dislikes and whether or not your preferred style would suit your home.

Some rooms have a built-in sense of style created by interesting original architectural features, while others have no personality at all once the contents are removed and the walls stripped for redecoration. The dullest room of all is the small box-shaped one with door, one or two small windows and no recesses or projections to provide interest. If you have a room with a strong architectural style, this may well dictate the type of decoration, furniture and furnishings you use. With a room lacking in character, you have the freedom to transform the room completely and create whatever atmosphere you feel is right.

Oberoi armchair (right)
designed by George J.
Sowden in 1981. A complete
room scheme can be
developed around one item of
furniture. Exotic Art Deco
bathroom (below) featuring
aquatic motifs.

*Simple but effective. Brilliantly
coloured furniture gives this
otherwise neutral room its
style* (right).

*Choosing and positioning
accessories is an integral part
of interior design. The elegant
collection* (below left) *adds
charm and interest to a
traditional bedroom. The
brightly coloured animals*
(below right) *cheekily
complement this unusual
bathroom window.*

TRADITIONAL

If you want to achieve a traditional atmosphere in a room in a modern or older home you will need to decorate it in a style relating to a specific historical period. Popular periods include Tudor, Georgian and Regency. Original or reproduction furniture, furnishings and accessories relating to these periods are available.

INGREDIENTS

Colours

Classical, in keeping with the relevant period – Adam greens, Wedgwood blues, Etruscan terracotta with black
Faded pastels, muted tones and neutrals for Regency, Georgian and other periods that were not overly ornate
Rich Oriental colours, intense jewel colours
Natural dyes for fabrics and furnishings

Furniture

Good antiques or reproduction furniture
Good wood pieces – tallboys, semi-circular tables, bureaux, chaise longues, dining tables and chairs and so on
Lavish or simply patterned upholstery according to the style of the period, brocade, velvet, silk, leather, embroidery
Classic shapes
Painted furniture featuring lacquering, gilding, stencilling or *trompe l'oeil*
Built-ins, such as bookcases decorated with mouldings, to suit the architectural style
Beds of the period – Empire four-posters or half-testers, for example
Brass inlaid pieces

Patterns

Will depend on the period and should be classical in origin
Gothic, Paisley, Oriental
Formal stripes and florals
Greek key, egg-and-dart, fleur de lys, Regency stripes

Textures

Carved and gilded opulence for Baroque
Smooth and matt with fine mouldings for classical and Georgian
Exotic woods and patterns as backgrounds to Chinese or African antiques
Simple natural textures to recreate Quaker and Shaker atmospheres

Walls

Patterned wall coverings, classical stripes or formal florals for Regency through to Baroque
Tapestry or draped fabric for an exotic look
Plain paint in eggshell or matt finish to set off classical cornices and fireplaces
Beading, panelling and border trims
Painting techniques – marbling, dragging, sponging and stippling – can enhance classical or rococo interiors

Ceilings

Decorative with ornate mouldings, cornices, coving, plasterwork
Painted scenes or cloudscapes for the more ornate traditional styles like Baroque, High Renaissance or rococo

Floors

A polished wood, inlaid woodblock or parquet floor is the essential element of authentic classical elegance
Marble floors and stairs are right for most restrained, classical interiors
Slate, flagstones, brick or tile are best suited to Tudor and Shaker styles
Tiles laid in chequerboard patterns embody Georgian and Edwardian interiors

Accessories

Gilt on opulent mirror and picture frames, highlighting simple Regency furniture, ornaments, antiquarian books and so on
Brass door handles, vases, beaten plates or even a Buddhist temple prayer gong according to traditional style chosen
Dark wood and Hogarth frames
Mirrors have to be chosen carefully – with wildly ornate gilded scrolls and fruit for a Baroque interior or simpler for Regency or Georgian interiors
China and glass, such as beautiful vases
Old Oriental pieces
Dramatic flower arrangements
Period lamps or chandeliers – plain for a Quaker room or with thousands of pendulous crystals for an ornate room
Flowering trees in tubs for an Orangerie effect
Oil paintings and/or early engravings and prints for a feeling of period

Classical colours — terracotta, gold and gilt — blend together the decoration and antique furniture of this traditionally designed hall (left). The sparse furniture, plain floorboards and delicate louvred shutters enhance rather than compete with the main decorative feature of this dining room — the elaborate 'trompe l'oeil' painting (below left). The architectural features of this grand bedroom — the cornices, picture rail and marble fireplace — are highlighted by the darker background colour and reflected in the carved wooden frame of the four poster.

COUNTRY HOUSE/RUSTIC

An elegant, simple and uncluttered style which is traditional in feel and romantic in atmosphere. The look is achieved by the casual but orderly placing of good-quality furniture and neat floral prints which, although smart, have a homely, relaxed feel to them. A link with natural elements through the use of cotton and wool for upholstery, wooden furniture and flowers and plants provide the country house with its style.

INGREDIENTS

Colours
Fresh and clear minty greens and blues, sunshine yellows
Soft pastels, muted as in watercolour painting, such as pale grey, pale blue, apricot, or rich, natural-dye shades of rust, terracotta, mushroom, creamy white
Faded Oriental

Furniture
Lovingly polished good wood pieces – chests of drawers, dressing tables, chairs, tables
Traditional pieces such as corner cupboards, refectory tables and settles
Provençal stripes and patterned loose covers
Knowle settees, Country-club chairs
Four-poster beds, alcove beds, half-testers
Bow-fronted chests of drawers
Blanket chests, library steps
Oriental lacquered pieces
Elegant stripped pine, not too rustic
Well-shaped, traditional mirrors

Patterns
Full-blown floral designs, cabbage rose patterns or drawn in botanical detail
Faded traditional
'Indoor conservatory'
Gothic
Traditional ethnic
Restrained stripes
Good patchwork

Textures
Rich and soft but not too opulent
Linens and restrained use of cotton or antique lace and broderie anglaise
Raw silks for upholstery and cushions
Cottons, voiles
Smooth woollen fabrics
Leather for books and upholstery
Polished wood, polished metal

Walls
Wood panelling or moulding
Patterned paper or fabric
Matt or semi-matt paint
Richly textured wall coverings

Ceilings
Some restrained decorative plasterwork
Paint
Beams

A
S
E
N
S
E

O
F

S
T
Y
L
E

Floors
Polished wood or parquet
Flagstone, brick or tile in kitchens or
    conservatories
Inlaid marble for entrance halls
Rush matting
Patterned and plain carpet
Oriental, hand-knotted or pegged rugs,
    classical and floral designs
Tiles laid in chequerboard patterns

Accessories
Silver, pewter, brass
Good-quality crystal
Dried flowers and grasses
Lace panels or trimming
Embroidered cushions
Displays of good-quality china
Prints, watercolours, oil paintings of
    landscapes, animals, portraits
Candlesticks, traditional lamps
Log baskets
Leather-bound books
Lace and patchwork bedcovers
Discreet chandeliers
Vases, collections of shells, miniatures or
    semi-precious stones
Flowers and plants

COTTAGE-STYLE

A country, rustic atmosphere is fairly
modest, simple in style but with character
and a certain appealing charm. Cottage style
above all has a lived in, natural character
with a fair amount of controlled clutter.

INGREDIENTS

Colours
Fresh and clean, pastels, natural or neutral
    colours
Muted and faded rich tones
Highlights of bright colour

Furniture
Simple wooden pine chests and washstands
Oak settles, Windsor chairs
Wooden rocking chairs, rush-seated,
    stick-back or bentwood chairs
Gate-legged or scrubbed pine kitchen tables

Patterns
Small and neat
Traditional or classical, such as mini-trellis
Mini-print florals
Patchwork, real and printed
Small-scale checks and stripes
Well-drawn florals
Delft-style tile designs

Textures
Simple, honest and homespun
Natural fibres, cotton, linen, wool, tweed
Weaves
Waxed wood
Copper, pewter, brass
Stone, wood, clay tiles, brick

Ceilings
Plain paint
Wood-clad or beamed

Floors
Polished wood boards, which are sometimes
    stencilled
Rush matting, brick, slate, quarry tiles
    cork, rag or woven rugs

Accessories
Earthenware
Brass candlesticks
Copper kettles
Dried and fresh flowers
Wooden implements
Prints of naive paintings
Crochet and patchwork cushions and bed
    covers
Iron latches
Collections of blue-and-white china, herbs,
    teapots, kettles, etc

Dried flowers and grasses against whitewashed brick, with stripped pine chest of drawers, wicker and brick floor are all essential ingredients of the rustic look (far left). Natural textures and handcrafted pieces form the basis of this country style room scheme (left). Geometric tiles add an unexpected splash of colour to a farmhouse kitchen, otherwise traditional in its wooden units, stone walls and hanging utensils (below far left). Framed photographs provide lively points of interest in an earth-coloured bedroom (below centre). Wood panelled walls in this entrance hall (below), seen from the front door, immediately give the visitor the impression of a country house on a grand scale.

VIGOROUS VICTORIAN

A rather heavy and sometimes florid style, which features a lot of gilt and brass, flock and chenille and intricate styling for upholstery. This style gives you a chance to be a little flamboyant or excessive with pattern. Treat ceilings dramatically and choose textures for their voluptuous feel.

INGREDIENTS

Colours
Rich, smouldering, deep, dark colours
Rich reds, golds, madonna blues, strong greens
Colours of natural dyes

Furniture
Heavy with ornate fretwork and other carved decoration
Dominating pieces for large rooms
Richly polished ebony, mahogany, walnut
Cane and bamboo
Wrought-iron combined with wood or glass
Wicker or cast iron furniture
Overstuffed upholstery with fringes, tassels and piping
Leather Chesterfields
Ornate brass or gilt trimmings
Suites of furniture
Brass or cast iron bedsteads

Patterns
Flowing, yet formal florals
Bold over-blown florals
Victorian Gothic geometrics
Wide, formal stripes
Botanically accurate plants such as acanthus

Textures
Opulent and very tactile: velvet, chenille, flock, lace, leather, intricately carved wood and cut crystal
Brass, gilt, iron, black lead
Mirror and etched glass
Leather, rattan and cane
Majolica ceramics

Walls
Patterned wall coverings of the period
Fabric clad, paint
Dado rails and panels
Heavy over-mantles above fireplaces
Border and frieze trims
Painting techniques such as marbling

Ceilings
Decorative plasterwork, mouldings, cornices
Wood panelling and beams

Floors
Tile, slate and flagstone kitchen floors
Polished or inlaid wood, parquet
Floral, Oriental, tapestry and rag rugs
Plain and patterned carpet
Marble
Linoleum, can be inlaid
Chequerboard and border effects

Accessories
Stained and etched glass
China and knick knacks
Green plants
Gilt and brass pictures, heavily-framed prints, samplers and lacework
Fruit and flowers or stuffed animals
Lamps made from converted gas or oil lamps
Fenders and fire irons
Embroidered fire screens and pictures
Assorted cushions

THE GRAND STYLE

A frankly flamboyant style, which has its roots in periods like the French Empire and rococo. This type of design can also be of Oriental, Indian or Turkish origin. Modern-day versions of the Grand Style can be great fun if used cleverly to give atmosphere and character to an uninspired room, using fake Greek columns and marbling in the bathroom, for example.

INGREDIENTS

Colours
Strong, rich, dark, jewel-bright and sharply contrasted
Black, white and rich natural colours, such as terracotta
Silver and gold used to define shapes and details

Furniture
Authentic to suit the particular period or reproduction
Painted or lacquered, fake finishes
Ethnic, Oriental
Gilt- and brass-trimmed
Coloured, patterned and tooled leather
Opulent upholstery
Heavy woods, often dark or richly coloured woods with an interesting grain

Patterns
Will depend on the origin of the ornamental or Baroque style
Traditional European, Chinese, Indian, Moorish
Strongly patterned surfaces can be mixed, if of similar origin
Some abstract or formal geometric
Classical

Textures
Light-filtering screens or fabrics
Exotic marbles, velvet, silk, satin, brocade contrasted with harsher metallic elements
Ceramics, leather, exotic woods
Lacquer and gilt
Shaggy and natural pile for rugs and fabrics

Walls
Patterned to suit style or period with paper, paint, mosaics, wall coverings
Fabric-covered or draped
Richly patterned rugs as wall-hangings
Trompe l'oeil, such as clouded skies
Panelling

Ceilings
Ornamental and exotic
Tented
Trompe l'oeil skies, views

Floors
Polished, stained, painted or inlaid wood
Marble, terrazzo, tile
Patterned or plain carpet
Oriental and ethnic rugs
Animal skin rugs, hand-woven rugs

Accessories
Unusual and exotic, opulent to suit scheme
Brass, gilt, silver and other metals
Large ethnic items, often spotlighted
Decorated woods
Stained glass

A highly atmospheric grand dining room (left), clothed from ceiling to floor with knotted rope hangings and strikingly furnished with fibre glass pyramid-shaped dining chairs and table and stone statuary. The clutter is housed elsewhere. This flamboyant bathroom (below far left) reminiscent of a grand Viennese café is all reflection — polished wood, gloss finish ceiling, huge mirrors and chandeliers. Oriental shapes and motifs (below centre) in an elaborate reception area. Intense and vibrant colours wherever you look — wall hangings, bed cover, window dressings and wall coverings create a rich, exhuberant atmosphere (below).

ELEGANT EDWARDIAN/ART NOUVEAU

The origins of modern interior design lie in Edwardian style. It looks back in time to the best of classical pattern, shape and form, and tries to recreate the purity of line using more modern materials. Art Nouveau style was inspired by the arching forms of plants. Its strongest feature is the whiplash motif which appears in Art Nouveau designs from textiles to mouldings. It is largely the furniture and choice of motifs in textiles and accessories that defines whether the finished room has an Edwardian or an Art Nouveau flavour, the style is in the details and colour coordination.

Ingredients

Colours

Pale but not pastel and subtly contrasted – generally light and airy, more 'modern' combinations for Art Nouveau, more 'traditional' for Edwardian
Jewel-rich
Natural dyes
Neutrals

Furniture

Arts and Crafts furniture for late Edwardian styles, largely in rich chestnut-coloured and lighter coloured woods
Carved wood - pared down elegant shapes

for Edwardian styles, flowing, sinuous shapes for Art Nouveau style
Well-painted pieces in Edwardian or Art Nouveau style
Streamlined functional items with interesting detail are largely Edwardian but some Art Nouveau pieces have small flower or stylized motifs
More traditional brass-trimmed pieces, such as Edwardian bureaux or bookcases
Simple oak and pine
Robust tables or sideboards
Delicate- or fragile-looking occasional chairs
Button-backed upholstery
Dramatic Mackintosh furniture or the more curvacious designs of Guimard

Patterns

William Morris textiles and Art Nouveau florals
Up-dated classical images
Geometrics
Designs based on natural forms
Sonia Delaunay and Eileen Grey geometrics

Textures

Basic and natural for simple schemes – linen, hessian, brick, stone, leather, wool, crocheted cotton or wool
More opulent for elegant rooms - silks, satins, velvets, brass, lace, cane and rattan
Good, polished wood - often light in colour, such as elm, oak and pearwood

Ceramics, china, glass
Tracery of wrought iron (less wrought iron for Art Nouveau style)

Walls

Wood panelling
Plain or decoratively painted
Paper in typical pattern of period
Fabric-clad

Ceilings

Beamed, wood-clad
Plain

Floors

Boards, inlaid parquet, woodblock
Tile, brick, flagstone
Plain or patterned carpet, rugs
Linoleum
Some marble

Accessories

Stained or etched glass
Screens
Lace
Plants
Fresh and dried flower arrangements
China or earthenware
Silver, pewter
Oil lamps
Brass and cast iron items
Marble and alabaster
Some Art Nouveau pieces
Statuettes

Gilt bronze lamps like this one portraying the American dancer Loïe Fuller epitomize Art Nouveau style. An Art Nouveau Parisian bedroom (above) designed by Hector Guimard is complete down to *the last detail. The furniture is of steamed pearwood. Many famous chair designs from the Art Nouveau and Art Deco periods, like this high-backed Mackintosh chair (right), are available as reproductions* *today. This Art Deco sitting room (below) features authentic period items — the fireplace, rug and table — and motifs such as the leaping gazelles.*

ART DECO

This style was a reaction to Art Nouveau and was an attempt to eliminate excessive decoration with items often designed for mass production. It was inspired in part also by the bright colours and more geometric designs of the costumes of the Ballets Russes when they appeared in Paris in the early 1900s and fulfilled the need for a new direction in design and the use of colour. Elements of Art Deco were used right through into the 1930s, typified by the glamour of ocean-going liners and the cinema.

INGREDIENTS

Colours
Fresh pastels - peach, light blue
Neutral and natural colours
White and off-white
Black, white and grey
Some rich, dark colours
Sharp accents
Some primary colours
Gold and silver

Furniture
Streamlined or swirling geometric shapes
'New' materials, such as metals, glass, early plastics like bakelite
Fur, leather, canvas used for upholstery
Printed and woven fabric loose covers
Unadorned wood
Painted items
Exotic woods, such as satinwood and bird's eye maple for bedroom suites

Patterns
Mostly structured geometrics but early Art Deco style includes sylph-like stylized women and floral or foliage motifs
Early abstracts

Textures
Opulent satin, silk, velvet
Glossy ceramic, glass, chrome, other metals
Matt and shaggy furs or pile carpet
Bleached and limed woods
Stained, ebonized items
Leather, wool tweed, canvas

Walls
Plain paint
Decoratively painted with wall patterns in geometric style, some murals
Patterned paper
Glass panels
Marble
Wood panels, natural or painted
Fabric-clad
Mirrors

Ceilings
Plain paint
Simple covings – some streamlined plasterwork
Beams
Illuminated

Floors
Stripped board
Tile, marble
Inlaid linoleum and sheet material
Cork, matting
Plain and patterned carpet
Rugs - especially large circular ones

Accessories
Decorative light fittings in glass or metal, the classic Art Deco design featuring a woman holding a lighted sphere
Glass and china figures, clocks
Statuary
Plants, distinctive flower arrangements
Satin cushions
Etched glass

MINIMAL/MODERN

The essence of this type of design relies on functionalism to provide the best possible results. It is a paring down of ornamentation until a streamlined, almost spartan interior is created, with everything in its alloted place. Simple, unadorned shapes have to be selected with care and the quality of all surfaces must be superb, even if some are textured and appear to be basic and unpretentious. Take as your guide the classic aesthetic simplicity of Japanese interiors.

Ingredients

Colours
Cool pastels
Neutrals
Natural colours for natural items
Some splashes of restrained primary colour

Furniture
Well-designed, functional items
Modern or traditional
Streamlined shapes
Practical multi-purpose or folding
Classical

Patterns

Should be confined to two or three surfaces
Classical or geometrical

Textures
Should be contrasting to add interest
Matt with shiny, shaggy or rough with
    smooth, chrome, brushed aluminium,
    mirrors or foil with ceramic finishes
Decorative woods
Some painted techniques used with restraint

Walls
Plain paint, painted textures
Wall coverings in suitable patterns
Fabric, wood or laminate-clad
Faced mirror or special decorative glass

Ceilings
Plain paint, painted textures
Decorated sparingly with mouldings
Wood-clad
Illuminated

Floors

Marble, tile
Wood of all types, cork
Plain, patterned or bordered carpet
Dhurries, hand-tufted specials and Oriental
    rugs
Sheet vinyl or linoleum, sometimes inlaid
Border effects
Smooth-textured and studded rubber
Finely woven sisals or mattings

Accessories
Artistic foliage plants, shrubs in pots
Impressive flower arrangements
Classic collections
Period antiques, carefully arranged
Well-lit modern painting or paintings,
    photographs and prints

This bedroom (top) is inspired by Japanese simplicity of line, the horizontals of the screen wall are reflected in the bed linen. Modern architectural style houses traditional furniture and floor covering in this airy and spacious sitting area (above). Minimal use of colour in a streamlined kitchen maximizes space (right).

Geometrics, curves, steel and plain expanses of colour are carefully chosen to create a supremely modern living environment (left). Furniture from le Corbusier (below left). Pattern is created by careful positioning of the framed prints, which reflect the structure of the furniture. 'Tilt' tables (below) look as if they are about to collapse. A modern setting is softened by the glow of an open fire (bottom).

HARD EDGE/HIGH TECH

This is a very streamlined and practical style of decorating and furnishing. It requires a basic but imaginative approach, often recycling products made originally for industrial use – for example, beds made from scaffolding, supermarket shelving adapted for home storage, flooring of studded rubber. Despite the use of industrial materials, this style can look comfortable and welcoming by choosing accessories and textiles cleverly.

Ingredients

Colours
Neutrals for the basic shell – whites, off-whites, greys, black, smoky-brown
Pastels used as neutrals or highlights
Bold or clever use of primaries

Furniture
Functional, streamlined
Items adapted from industry and retail, such as metal shelving and plastic containers
Metal, canvas or plastic
Basic woods, such as black ash

Patterns
Should be almost non-existent
Some stripes
Graph-like checks
Linear, geometric, abstract

Textures
Should be strongly contrasted: matt with gloss, rough or shaggy with smooth

Walls
Plain paint
Heavily textured (natural)
Wood-clad
Brick or stone
Cork
Hessian, canvas, wool weave
Some patterned wall coverings or abstract painted wall patterns
Laminate- or ceramic-clad

Ceilings
Plain paint
Wood-clad
Metal, laminate, tile-clad
Lowered and illuminated

Floors
Natural materials
Plain and studded rubber
Wood
Sheet material – linoleum or vinyl
Cork
Industrial flooring
Tile
Some modern carpets or rugs

Accessories
Should be limited and functional
Functional lighting often borrowed from industrial sources
Light fitting as 'art form'
Unadorned flowers in simple geometric containers
Houseplants, largely of the aesthetic foliage kind
Modern glass
Statuary
Books or magazines
Modern crockery

High tech luxury. A monochromatic bathroom (left) features chrome fine-slatted blinds, black accessories and invisible storage. A glass house with skeletal steel structure reflects nature back at itself (far left). Open-plan living for a modern age — slatted blinds screen sleeping area from sitting area (bottom far left). Cleverly alternated pastel colours create a warm and inviting atmosphere in the conversation area of this spacious house (below).

A
S
E
N
S
E

O F

S T Y L E

ECLECTIC

This look is for those who like a variety of styles and buy accordingly. It works when bits and pieces are put together cleverly, mixing old with new, taking great care to get the look right in unexpected juxtapositions. The furniture and backgrounds can be simple, with all the interest created by means of the accessories, although clever wall paintings, collages and craft objects can be an integral part of the eclectic style. It is a style for the individual, with no hard or fast rules as to what is right or wrong.

INGREDIENTS

Colours
Brash and bright in original combinations, ethnic, neutral, clashing, contrasting, toning, graduated or dark and rich to suit the room and your particular set of furniture

Furniture
Almost anything goes and styles can be mixed together
Leather
Wood
Glass
Chrome and other metals
Canvas chairs
Over-stuffed upholstery
Over-decorated items
Streamlined pieces
Kitsch items adapted and used as furniture - juke box, sewing machine treadle table
Triple mirrors as bedhead
Modern classics like Mackintosh, Le Corbusier and Mies van der Rohe chairs or tables

Patterns
Art Deco
Art Nouveau
1920s and 1930s geometrics
Ethnic

1940s and 1950s contemporary
Animal skins

Textures
Rough, harsh, homespun
Shiny, matt
Opulent or metallic,

Walls
Patterned wall coverings
Fabrics
Plain painted
Decoratively painted
Covered with collections or posters
Trompe l'oeil
Collage
Bare or textured plaster

Ceilings
Decorative and beamed
Painted plain or with special techniques
Clad with tile or trellis
False and illuminated

Floors

Wood
Cork
Tile
Plain or patterned carpet
Painted plain or patterned (solid or wood)
Geometric or fairly sparsely patterned
    modern rugs
Rubber
Linoleum
Sheet vinyl

Accessories

These are a mixture of all types, modern and
    traditional, and should be massed
    together in a collection
Paintings
Sculptures
Vases
Uplighters, wall lights, spotlights

*An Art Deco dressing table is
effectively blended in with
pastel coloured modern
bedroom furnishings (above).
Fruit cup fabric from Warner
and Sons (far left) would
provide interest, contrast and
colour in any eclectic
collection of soft furnishings.
A pink boomerang-shaped
table is just one of many
unusual items collected
together in this startling
sitting area (centre left
above). A small corner of the
1950s is created by zebra
pattern, mirror surface, colour
and period artefacts (left).*

SECTION FIVE

DIRECTORY OF MATERIALS

A comprehensive range of types of paint, fabric, wall covering, flooring and lighting fixture is presented in chart form in this section. The charts also indicate what type of surface or purpose a particular material is suitable for.

Before buying any materials, make sure you calculate the quantity required accurately, allowing for a certain amount of wastage. If you are buying an expensive item, such as quarry tiles for a large area, take advantage of any measuring facilities offered by the store. In the case of quarry tiles, for example, it is difficult for the non-expert to estimate how many additional tiles will be needed for going round corners and into cupboards. Whatever you are buying – wallpaper, paint or fabric – it is essential to buy enough materials to complete the job at the beginning. Paint colours, fabric dyes and tile colours will vary from batch to batch and you can never guarantee finding more of the same batch if you run out halfway through the job.

FLOOR COVERINGS

Hard floors

Any hard flooring must be laid on the correct subfloor, which should be strong, level, clean, smooth and damp-proof. Many hard floors, such as floorboards, are pre-existing and can be refurbished as long as they are in good condition (see page 144).

Most of the floorings in this section are difficult to lay and are best left to the professionals, although some of the wood floors can be successfully laid by a do-it-yourself enthusiast.

Bricks and paving are mainly used for patios, conservatories and garden rooms. They are also found in older properties on the ground floor, laid directly on to the earth. They come in natural, attractive brick colours and patterns and borders can be formed. The herringbone method of laying is most commonly found.

Ceramic tiles come in different sizes, shapes and thicknesses. They are used on floors in bathrooms, kitchens, utility rooms and garden extensions or conservatories. They may be found in halls in older properties. Most types are glazed and are impervious to water and most liquids. Make sure you choose floor or multi-purpose tiles — wall tiles are not strong enough. Select frost-proof tiles if necessary for patios, balconies, sun rooms and conservatories. These are very heavy, so check how much weight the joists can take before installing them upstairs.

Flagstones are found in some older properties on the ground floor. Again they may be laid directly on earth and can be restored and sealed.

Floorboards are already laid upstairs and downstairs in many types of house. If they are in good condition (see page 144 for comments/repair) they can be sanded and sealed, stencilled, painted plain or patterned with floor paint, stained and sealed or treated to one of the special painting techniques such as marbling.

Marble is used particularly in elegant European-style properties and in some old traditional houses. It comes in several attractive, natural colours and in many different shapes and sizes. It can be laid plain or in unusual or traditional patterns. Marble is heavy so check that the joists can take the weight before laying upstairs.

Mosaics can be made up of glass, marble or ceramic pieces, usually slightly irregular in shape. Some come with a paper or mesh backing in a 15cm/6in square for ease of laying. Mosaic pictures or patterns should be planned in advance and laid individually. Mosaics, like marble, are heavy so check that the joists can take the weight before installing upstairs.

Slate is a quarried material and comes in grey-green and other natural colours. It is available in random shapes or as paving slabs. It is very heavy and has to be embedded in a cement or concrete subfloor. It is too heavy for use upstairs.

Stone is not used much nowadays, although it is found on the ground floor of some older properties. It comes in many different colours and thicknesses and many areas have a local stone. It is usually square or rectangular. Some types need sealing before laying, and again stone is a heavy material to use.

Terrazzo is usually made from marble chippings and is ground or polished. It is set in cement or polyester resin. Colour, texture and shape vary, although it is usually sold in square or rectangular slab form. Again it is a heavy material to use.

Wood floors include woodblock, hardwood strip and parquet, as well as floorboards. Different types of wood are used, and shapes and sizes vary according to the product. Prices also vary according to thickness and timber used. Wood floors can be a very decorative and elegant flooring and once sealed are easy to look after.

Semi-hard floors

Like hard floors, semi-hard floors are usually stuck to the subfloor. Poor floorboards can be covered with a hardboard or flooring-grade chipboard, rough side down to give a level surface and to assist adhesion of the new flooring, which must be level, smooth and damp-proof.

All these types of flooring can be laid by a professional or an competent amateur.

Cork tiles normally come in natural golden-brown tones, but are also available in different colours. Size and shape vary, and they can be laid in a chequerboard pattern or border effect. Cork is resilient and warm underfoot, and should be sealed — the pre-sealed type is best for kitchens and bathrooms where there is a damp atmosphere and where spills might occur.

Linoleum is an old-fashioned flooring currently enjoying a revival. Colours are generally muted and often marbled, but other bolder patterns are also available. It comes in sheet or tile form. Inlaid patterns are possible with either type. Different thicknesses are available. Old linoleum can be refurbished and polished or sealed if it is in good condition.

Rubber is very bouncy underfoot and cuts down noise. It comes in tile or sheet form in a range of subtle colours. Textured types are non-slip. It is generally used as commercial flooring.

Thermo-plastic tiles are thin, plastic tiles, square or rectangular in shape, usually available in soft, subtle colours with a slightly marbled texture. They are more often found in recent properties. They can be laid in interesting patterns and designs.

Semi-soft floors

These are soft and flexible underfoot but are usually stuck to the subfloor, although some are 'laid flat' and only require stapling or fixing down where there are doorways, or where they are likely to be kicked up. These floorings can be equally well laid by a professional or a competent amateur.

Cushioned vinyl comes in sheet form of various widths and several thicknesses. The vinyl has air bubbles trapped between the wear layer and the backing which gives the flooring thickness and bounce. It is available in many designs and patterns — often simulating other traditional floorings such as wood, ceramic tiles or slate, with varying degrees of success.

Sheet vinyl and vinyl tiles are thinner, more brittle versions of cushioned vinyl. Many of the tiles are self-adhesive and they are very simple to lay.

Soft floor coverings

These include carpets, rugs and mattings and are made from various fibres. They are usually fitted directly on to the subfloor, or loose-laid on top of any of the hard, semi-hard and semi-soft floors detailed above.

Fitted carpets should be professionally laid, especially on staircases. Carpet squares, rugs and loose-laid tiles can be tackled by the amateur. All fitted carpet needs a good underlay — never lay new carpet on old underfelt or old carpet. Sometimes this is built-in in the form of heavy foam backing, otherwise you will have to buy it separately. There are many kinds of underlay available — felt, foam, rubber, PVC, latex — and you will need to take advice on what suits your floor covering.

Axminster carpet is made up of cut pile tufts placed in position as the backing is woven. Fibres and blends of fibre vary and different pile effects can be produced. Many colours and patterns are available and they come in narrow widths, broadloom (made on a wide loom) and as carpet squares.

Bonded carpets are made by bonding a sheet of surface pile on to a backing and cutting the pile afterwards. The fibres are usually synthetic and can be blended with other materials. The colours are usually plain and the widths are broadloom.

Needlefelt/needlepunch carpets can have a texture like cord or felt and are usually made with synthetic fibre. Different patterns and colours are available and widths vary.

Tufted carpets are made by placing tufts into a woven backing and securing on the reverse side with a latex coating. The fibres and blends of fibres vary. They are available in different widths and plain or patterned colours. Tufted rugs including some hand-tufted are also available.

Wilton carpets. The surface pile of Wilton carpets is woven in a continuous thread with the backing for strength and taken to the base when a new colour is included. Fibres and blends of fibre vary, but Wiltons often contain some wool. The pile can be textured, plain (velvet) or carved. They come in plain or multi-colours and are available as widths for seaming for fitted carpets, broadloom and squares.

Carpet tiles can be made by any of the above methods with different synthetic fibres and blends of fibre. They come in plain or patterned designs and different sizes and textures. They are often backed for loose-laying.

Matting is harsher underfoot than carpet. It is usually made of natural fibres like sisal, hemp, rush, coir or hair. The colours are also generally natural, although some mattings are dyed. They may be seamed and fitted, broadloom and fitted, or bound and used as rugs.

Rugs can be woven by hand or machine-made by the various methods described under carpets. Rugs originate from many different countries, and those from the East or Orient can be particularly valuable. They include Afghans, Berbers, Bokharas, Chinese (hand-washed Chinese), Dhurries, Kelims, Numdahs and Persian. European and American rugs include rag rugs, Rya, hand-pegged, hand-tufted and tapestry. Colours and patterns are infinitely varied as are sizes, shapes and textures. Rugs will usually be placed on top of one of the other floorings. Underfelt is unnecessary, but ensure that rugs placed on a polished floor have a non-slip backing.

PAINT

There are two basic types of paint — oil- or resin-based and water-based. When you buy paint always read the small print on the can to make sure it is the right paint for the job, and check the coverage and whether any undercoat or preparation is needed. When undercoat is recommended, use one in the colour recommended made by the same manufacturer. If you have a large area to cover, make sure you buy paint with the same batch number because the colour may vary slightly from batch to batch. If paint is being mixed to achieve a special shade, get all the paint you will need mixed at one time.

Emulsion is a water-based paint with either a matt finish or a slight sheen. It is used for internal walls and ceilings, and is also available for external use. It is available as free-flowing or gel (non-drip). New developments include textured emulsions and solid emulsion which comes in a block and is particularly useful for painting ceilings.

Eggshell/lustre is an oil-based paint with a matt or semi-matt surface. It can be used for woodwork and metalwork inside and on interior walls. It is available as free-flowing or gel (non-drip).

Gloss is an oil-based paint with a shiny surface. It is used on walls, wood and metal both inside and outside. It is available as free-flowing or gel (non-drip). Most gloss paints require a special undercoat.

Masonry paint is a tough emulsion specially formulated for use on exterior walls. Most masonry paints contain a mould and algae inhibitor, and some have additives to improve coverage and durability. It creates a textured surface.

Microporous paint is solvent- or water-based and allows the wooden surface to which it is applied to breathe. It has a gloss finish and is suitable for exterior use. It is highly flexible and cracking and blistering are unlikely to occur. It should be applied to a

	OLD SURFACE	PLASTER PLASTERBOARD	BUILDING BOARD e.g. wallboard, hardboard, insulation board	GLOSS PAINT	EGGSHELL PAINT	MULTI-PURPOSE PAINT	
PREPARATION		Make sure new plaster has dried out or use a paint which allows plaster to 'breathe', over stabilizing primer. Wash/rub down if necessary. Tape joints and line plasterboard	Tape joints and line	Clean down, remove any perished paint, rub down, patch prime if necessary. Apply the recommended undercoat. If using gloss on top of eggshell, rub down with wet and dry.			
NEW COAT	GLOSS PAINT	n/r	n/r	✓	✓	✓	
	EGGSHELL PAINT	✓	✓	✓	✓	✓	
	MULTI-PURPOSE PAINT	✓	✓	✓	✓	✓	
	MATT OR SILK EMULSION PAINT	✓	✓	'Key' with sandpaper or wet and dry first to provide a suitable surface.		✓	
	WATER BOUND PAINT e.g. distemper	not vinyl emulsion	n/r	△	△	△	

freshly-primed surface. No undercoat is required.

Multi-purpose paint is oil-based and can be used on wood and metalwork as well as ceilings and walls inside the home. It has a gloss or semi-gloss finish and contains silicone and polyurethane, making it tough and flexible. It has the added advantage that paintbrushes can be washed out under the tap.

Primer is a special type of paint, formulated to protect new or exposed wood or metal surfaces. This is applied before the undercoat or topcoat. Stabilizing primers are also available for sealing damp, flaking walls.

Textured paint is water-based and gives a thick, gritty texture to walls and ceilings. It is usually applied with a roller or special spreader. Once applied it can be difficult to remove.

Tinted paint comes in a wide range of colours. The tinting system involves mixing paints together. They are oil-based or water-based and come in gloss, lustre, matt and silk vinyl finishes. Different cans of base coat paint are kept by the supplier. For each colour shade, pigment is added to the relevant base coat and shaken mechanically.

Undercoat is oil-based and is specially formulated for use with oil-based top-coat paint for woodwork and metal. Always use undercoat and top coat paint from the same manufacturer to ensure the correct shade.

The chart below indicates what paint is suitable for what surface, and what preparation the old surface requires before redecorating. (Information in the chart courtesy of Crown Paints Limited.)

KEY TO CHART

n/r	not recommended
△	not suitable
✓	suitable

MATT OR SILK EMULSION PAINT	WATER BOUND PAINT e.g. distemper	RELIEF & EMBOSSED WALL COVERINGS e.g. Anaglypta	WALLPAPERS VINYL WALL COVERINGS	HESSIAN	SPECIALITY WALL COVERINGS e.g. grass-cloth
Wash down, 'key' if necessary. Use a thinned coat of emulsion if necessary or undercoat if recommended.	If non-powdery type, wash down several times with warm, soapy water to remove loose material. Apply one coat stabilizing primer before repainting. If powdery type, all old material *must* be removed. Reline walls and ceilings if necessary.	Make sure these are sticking firmly to the wall and no paste has been left on the surface.	Make sure the wall covering is sticking firmly and no paste is on the front of paper. If paper has boldly coloured or gold/silver pattern, test first. If necessary, remove it and re-line the wall. Some hand-printed papers can also 'bleed' through paint, so test first.		Make sure the wall covering is sticking firmly to the wall and no paste has been left on. Dust down before you start decorating.
✓	n/r	but can be difficult to strip	n/r	n/r	n/r
✓	✓	✓	✓	n/r	n/r
✓	✓	✓	✓	n/r	n/r
✓	✓	✓	✓	✓	n/r
△	✓	n/r	n/r	n/r	n/r

WALL COVERINGS

A wide range of wall coverings is available in paper, vinyl and fabric and in many different colours, patterns and textures. They can be divided into two categories — flexible and rigid.

Always buy enough wall covering to complete the job, allowing for wastage. Make sure that all rolls or lengths have the same batch number, because the colour or shading may vary from batch to batch. Unwrap all rolls and check before starting to decorate.

Flexible wall coverings

Lining paper is used to give a smooth base layer either for other wall coverings or for paint. If another wall covering is to be hung over the top, the lining paper is hung horizontally — this is called cross-lining. If the wall is to be painted, it is hung vertically.

Standard printed wallpaper comes in a wide range of patterns, colours and textures in standard rolls. Some types are washable and some are ready-pasted.

Hand-blocked or hand-painted wallpapers are available with exclusive and expensive designs. Special designs can be commissioned. Some of these papers are not colour-fast so they will need professional handling.

Borders and friezes are narrow bands of paper or vinyl wall covering used to outline features like picture rails or to form decorative divisions. They can be coordinated with wall coverings or with plain painted walls.

Ingrain or woodchip is a white wallpaper with wood or other chippings incorporated into the pulp to give it a textured finish. It is hung vertically and overpainted. It is particularly useful for concealing defective wall surfaces.

Embossed wall coverings are also relief wall coverings or 'whites'. They are made from white compressed paper/pulp to form a heavily textured surface which can cover many imperfections or uneven plastering. They come in many textures and are hung in the same way as wallpaper and then overpainted. Some heavy types are sold in panels. Embossed vinyls are also available.

Vinyl wall coverings come in a wide range of styles and textures. They basically consist of a vinyl layer incorporating the plain colour or pattern, which is then printed on to a paper backing or fabric backing. The fabric backed vinyls are particularly suitable for kitchens and bathrooms because they are highly water repellent. A heavy texture to create the illusion of fabric can be incorporated. All are durable and washable, and some are ready-pasted and easy-strip. Heavy 'contoured' or 'blown' vinyl wall coverings are also produced, sometimes simulating ceramic tiles or natural textures. Vinyl is usually sold by the roll, but some fabric-backed ones are sold by the metre/yard.

Foamed polyethylene is a lightweight and porous wall covering and is hung like wallpaper. The wall is pasted and not the back of the polyethylene. Different designs and colours are available and companion borders are also produced.

Foils or metallics are made from metallized plastic film on a paper backing. They are hung like paper using fungicidal paste. Light switches or power points should not be placed over foils or metallics.

Flocked wall coverings have a velvety texture. They come as paper or vinyl and some are ready-pasted. The designs and colours are suitable for traditional schemes.

Fabric can be used to cover walls and ceilings. Some fabrics are specially treated and made extra-wide for this purpose. The types of fabric that can be used are numerous and include burlap, upholstery fabric, velvet and even silk. They can be stuck, stapled, battened on or fixed by special track to the wall. They are normally sold by the metre/yard or if paper-backed by the roll. For detailed instructions on fixing fabric to the wall see page 128.

Upholsterer's hessian can be fixed to walls as fabric, but it is usually stuck to a pasted wall. Paper-backed hessian is hung like paper. A range of rich colours, rarely patterned, is available. The fabric is sold by the metre/yard and the paper-backed hessian is sold by the roll.

Felt can be obtained in many colours and can be used to cover walls. It can be fixed as fabric. Special paper-backed felts are also produced and are hung like paper. Felt is sold as fabric by the metre/yard or paper-backed by the roll.

Suede and woven textile coverings are both produced with a paper backing and hung like wallpaper. They come in a wide range of colours and the woven textile coverings have a textured finish. They are normally sold in rolls but occasionally by the metre/yard.

Natural textures include grasscloths and cork. Again they are usually paper-backed and hung as paper. They are sold by the roll or by the metre/yard.

Rigid wall coverings

Ceramic tiles are available in a very wide range of styles, sizes, patterns, colours and even textures. They are usually glazed to make them impervious to water, steam and condensation. Tiles are fixed to the wall with adhesive and the gaps between the tiles are grouted. Some tiles have several glazed edges, and are self-spacing to make fixing easier. They are usually sold by the square metre/yard. Mosaic wall tiles are available already spaced on a flexible mesh backing.

Cork is available in tiles and panels, or bonded on to paper. It comes in both natural and dyed colours and has an attractive texture. It is ideal for wall areas or just for pinboards and provides good sound insulation. It is fixed in position with tile adhesive and should be sealed if the area is steamy or damp. It is sold either by the square metre/yard or as single packs of tiles.

Mirror/mirror tiles are available as panels, individual tiles and mosaics. Sizes vary considerably and some mirror glass is coloured, textured, patterned or etched. The tiles often come with adhesive pads or they can be battened on to the wall. The surface to be covered must be smooth or flat to avoid distortion of image. Mirror is sold by the square metre/yard or as individual panels.

Plastic laminates are available in a variety of colours, patterns and textures. Some are made to simulate brick, stone, ceramic tiles or wood. Alternatively fabrics can be laminated to allow for coordinated schemes. Laminate is usually bonded on to a backing, such as chipboard, to form panels and is either fixed or battened on to the wall. It is very useful for covering up old tiles or a poor surface. Some pre-formed panels which lock together are also available for bathrooms and kitchens. Sold by the square metre/yard or as panels.

Wood cladding/panelling comes in several forms. It is available as panels or tongue and grooved planks which fit neatly together. Woods and colours vary, but usually wood has to be stained and sealed, oiled or wax polished after hanging. Wood is usually fixed by means of battens and secret nailing but it can be stuck with contact adhesive. It is usually sold by length or by the panel.

Other rigid wall coverings such as brick, slate and stone can also be used. They either come as wall facings, or in their 'raw' state. Most are difficult to put up and will need professional fittings.

FABRICS

Furnishing fabrics are made from various natural, synthetic and combination fibres. Natural fibres are those made from vegetable and animal materials, such as wool, silk and cotton. Synthetic fabrics, such as acrylic and polyester, are produced by mixing chemicals with raw materials. Some fibres are more versatile than others, and at the moment there is no one particular fabric or fibre which can be used in every situation. When selecting a fabric, consider the job it has to do and the amount of wear it will get.

KEY TO CHART

n/r	not recommended
✓	suitable
△	but can crease

FABRIC TYPE	BED COVERS	CURTAINS AND DRAPES	CUSHIONS AND ACCESSORIES	LOOSE COVERS AND TAILORED COVERS	TABLECLOTHS/COVERS	UPHOLSTERY	OTHER
NATURAL FIBRES							
COTTON	✓△	✓	✓	— 100% cotton	✓	100% for very light use otherwise n/r	
LINEN	✓	✓	✓	— as linen/cotton union	✓	n/r	
SILK	✓	✓	✓		✓	n/r	
WOOL	✓	✓	✓		✓	✓	
SYNTHETIC FIBRES							
ACETATE	✓	✓	✓	n/r	✓	n/r	
ACRYLIC	✓	✓	✓	n/r	✓	✓	
MODACRYLIC	✓	✓	✓	n/r	✓	✓	
POLYESTER	✓	✓	✓	n/r	✓	— in suitable blend	High flame resistance so suitable for public use
MODIFIED POLYESTER (e.g. Trevira c.s.)	✓	✓	✓	n/r	✓	— in suitable blend	Bed linens
TERYLENE	✓	✓	✓	n/r	✓	n/r	High flame resistance
VISCOSE	✓	✓	✓	n/r	✓	✓	Net drapes, blinds, etc

LIGHTING FIXTURES

Dimmer switches are simple controls which are an alternative to domestic light switches. They increase or decrease the level of lighting at the turn of a knob or the touch of a plate. Dimmer fittings are also available as multiple units which control several circuits. They have a wattage limit, and should not be overloaded with too many fittings. Dimmers provide flexible, mood lighting and at the same time are energy-saving.

Downlighters are circular light fittings which can be recessed, semi-recessed or ceiling mounted to throw pools of light on to the surface below. They can be fitted with various types of bulb — flood, spot or ordinary incandescent. Most downlighters are anti-glare.

Fluorescent lights are tubular or circular fittings of various sizes. Slimline, miniature tubes are ideal for concealed lighting. Fluorescent lighting is operated by special controls, which makes fittings bulky and awkward, but has the advantage of being long lasting. The light produced can be cool or warm-white, but tends to be colder and more glaring than incandescent light. A recent development is the miniature, energy-saving fluorescent light bulb which is compactly shaped to fit into conventional lamps. This bulb needs an adaptor, and because it is more bulky than an ordinary bulb, a change of shade may be necessary if it is being fitted into an existing lamp.

Framing projectors are a domestic adaptation of theatrical lighting and can be shuttered to provide an accurate beam of light. They are ideal for highlighting pictures or displays.

Incandescent lamps are conventional filament bulbs, also known as tungsten. They can be pearlized, plain or coloured and come with bayonet or screw fittings. They give a warmer light than fluorescent lamps.

Low-vo'age bulbs give a precise beam and are particularly suitable for spot, flood and pinpoint lighting. When connected to normal voltage systems, they have to be channelled through a transformer. The transformer is often incorporated into the fitting and is neat and small.

Neon sculptures or tubes come in a variety of colours and can be shaped to form a decorative light or lamp. They can also be shaped to follow contours and used to frame a window or mirror, or outline a handrail or beam.

Reflector bulbs are incandescent light bulbs with a reflector coating. They are ideal for direct lighting because they give a stronger beam than a conventional bulb for the same wattage. They are available for most fittings. Conventional spotlight bulbs are usually of this type.

Rise-and-fall fittings are designed for ceiling lamp or pendant fittings, and enable the lamp to be moved up and down at will. The cable is stored within the fitting, and plays out and reels back as the lamp is pushed up or pulled down.

Tungsten-halogen lamps were originally developed for car headlamps and give out a small, concentrated light. They provide very powerful light from very small fittings. They must be handled with care so that the quartz envelope is not damaged. It is important not to touch the actual bulb with your fingers. Halogen lamps can be used with dimmer controls, but check with an electrician or lighting expert, because the rated wattage of dimmer equipment must be doubled if low voltage tungsten halogen fittings are installed.

Track lighting enables one electric outlet to supply several fittings which are plugged into the track. Tracks are most widely used for spotlights, but other lamps can be used if they have the correct plug-in fittings. Tracks can be recessed or surface mounted, and positioned across the ceiling, down walls or along skirtings. They can be fixed to form squares, oblongs and even circles and the fittings can usually be angled in several directions.

Uplighters throw light upwards, providing a dramatic accent light. They can be placed on floors, in amongst plants or on shelves.

Wallwashers are literally designed to 'wash a wall' with light and colour, and will make a room seem much more spacious. They are usually fixed about 1-1.5m/3-5ft away from the wall, ceiling mounted, but they can be placed closer to the wall if you want to use them to illuminate a collection of paintings or other wall decorations. In a large room, several wallwashers will be needed to achieve the correct balance of light.

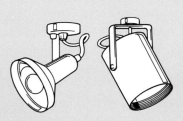

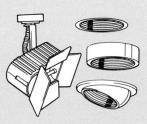

GLOSSARY

ACCENT A contrasting colour, often provided by **ACCESSORIES**, to brighten a decorative scheme, to add interest or to highlight. Accents may also be used to calm down a garish scheme.

ACCESSORY An accessory can be a cleverly displayed collection, a picture, books, cushions, china and glass or house plants. Accessories add interest to a room scheme, and can be chosen to soften or emphasize the style. Accessories often provide the colour **ACCENTS** in a room.

ADJACENT COLOURS A colour theory term which describes colours found next to each other on a **COLOUR WHEEL.**

ADVANCING COLOURS Colours which appear to come towards you – strong, warm colours, such as red, orange and yellow.

ALCOVE A vaulted recess in the wall of a room. An alcove may have an arched or a squared top.

ARCHITRAVE A moulded or decorative band framing a door, window or panel in a room.

ANTIQUING A process used to age wood and other surfaces artificially, achieved with paint, glazes and washes which are then 'distressed' to give them a worn appearance.

BALL-AND-CLAW FOOT A foot of a piece of furniture in the shape of a bird's claw or lion's paw holding a ball between its talons/claws. It was much used in the eighteenth century, and later copied by the Victorians.

BALUSTER A pillar used to support the handrail of a staircase, also called a bannister.

BEADING A narrow **MOULDING** of wood or plaster used to trim a deeper moulding, panel, frame or wall. Beading is used to simulate panels on doors and walls and to create a **DADO** rail.

BRIGHTNESS Applied to colour, brightness means highly saturated – vivid or strong.

CAFE CURTAINS Two or more rows of curtains, suspended one above the other across a window, usually on rods. They were originally seen in French and Belgian cafés, where they provided some privacy but enticed would-be customers with a glimpse of an attractive interior.

COLOUR BOARD A piece of board with samples of the components of a decorative scheme attached.

COLOUR WHEEL A method of showing the colours of the spectrum and how the three primary colours mix to form secondary and tertiary colours. Colours on one side of the wheel are cool and on the other side warm. The colour wheel also demonstrates the relationship between **COMPLEMENTARY** colours and **ADJACENT** colours.

COMBING A painting technique in which a wet layer of paint or **GLAZE** is 'teased' with the rigid teeth of a comb, to produce a striped effect or to simulate **WOOD GRAINING.**

COMPLEMENTARY COLOURS Pairs of colours which appear opposite each other on the **COLOUR WHEEL**, for example red and green, of which one is **RECEDING** (cool) and the other **ADVANCING** (warm). If two complementary colours are used in equal proportions, the advancing colour will appear to dominate.

CORBEL A projection from an interior or exterior wall which supports a beam, **MOULDING** or **CORNICE**. In older properties, these are often extravagantly decorated.

CORNICE A decorative horizontal band of plaster, wood or metal, used to trim the top of a wall where it meets the ceiling, or to conceal curtain fixtures or lighting fittings.

COVING Frequently preformed and added at a later stage than the original building/decoration, coving is similar to a **CORNICE**, but usually simpler in form.

DADO A wall treatment where the lower part is separated from the upper part by a horizontal rail or **BEADING** (the dado rail), or even a wallpaper border or **FRIEZE**. The lower part is usually treated differently from the upper, frequently panelled or covered with a heavily textured wall covering.

DRAGGING or **DRAGGED PAINTWORK** A painting technique used on walls and woodwork, where an almost dry brush is dragged across a surface to texture it.

FRAMING PROJECTOR A projector with shutters, developed from theatrical barn door lighting techniques, which enables an item to be skilfully lit.

FRIEZE A horizontal band around the walls of a room, usually positioned below the cornice or ceiling and above a picture rail. The term is also used to describe a narrow strip of wallpaper positioned horizontally.

GLAZE The application of a transparent or semi-transparent colour over another colour to enrich and intensify it. Glazing is part of the painting technique, glazing and wiping, where the glaze is applied and then wiped with a cloth or 'distressed' with another tool or fabric to create an interesting texture.

GRAINING A painting technique which imitates the grain and knots in wood, and is used to make a poor quality wood appear more expensive or to give another surface, such as heavily textured paper, the appearance of wood. Graining can be achieved in several ways, including **DRAGGING, RAGGING, COMBING** or **SCUMBLING.**

GROUT A filling worked into the gaps between tiles to create a flush surface.

HARMONY A mixture of colours which creates a pleasing effect.

HUE Pure colour – the attribute of colour which distinguishes it from another colour. The colours on the basic **COLOUR WHEEL** (primary, secondary and tertiary) are hues.

JAMB The side posts of a door, window or fireplace.

LAMINATE A tough surface material formed by pressing together layers of different substances. It is used to clad walls and to face furniture, kitchen units and so on.

'LIVE' PLASTER Plaster which has begun to crumble and which breaks up under pressure. The only successful treatment is to cut it out and replaster, building up in layers if necessary.

MARBLING A decorative finish which imitates marble, usually achieved with paint. High quality marbling can be difficult to distinguish from the real thing. Printed marbled effects are produced on wallpapers and fabrics.

MOIRE A wavy texture on fabric, which gives a watered effect (also called watered silk).

MONOCHROMATIC A term used to describe a colour scheme based on different **VALUES** of one colour, from light through to very dark.

MOULDING Decorative plasterwork or **BEADING** used on ceilings, woodwork, panelling or around window frames and doors.

NEUTRAL A term used to describe a colour without colour. The true neutrals are black, white and grey, but in interior design terms, fawn, beige, off-white and cream are also described as neutral. Items which take their colour from natural sources, such as stone, wood, sand and slate, are considered as neutrals, as are some simple striped and checked-effect patterns.

NEWEL POST The core of a winding or spiral stair-post, used at the top and bottom of a stair rail.

OVERMANTLE Ornamental shelving, sometimes incorporating a mirror, placed on top of a mantlepiece above a fireplace.

PAPIER MACHE Moulded paper pulp, used either to make solid objects which are then decorated or to fill gaps between floorboards to prevent dust rising.

PIGMENT Colouring matter – the essential ingredient added to paint to obtain the required colour.

POINTILLISM A method of designing or painting with dots, usually using the pointed end of an instrument, to suggest form and to produce a soft focus look.

PRISM A figure whose two ends are similar, equal and parallel and whose sides are parallelograms. The transparent or glass version usually has triangular ends, and when white light is passed through it, the light divides to form the colours of the spectrum.

RAG-ROLLING A painting technique which creates a textured effect by applying a base coat, allowing it to dry and applying a second coat or **GLAZE** with crumpled-up rags dipped in colour.

RECEDING COLOURS Colours which appear to go away from you, creating an impression of space and apparently increasing the size of the surface on which they are used, particularly in their palest **VALUES**. Receding colours are from the cool side of the **COLOUR WHEEL** - blue, green and violet.

RELIEF DECORATION A heavily textured surface where part of the design stands out from the background in relief. Some wall coverings have a relief design and a raised and textured surface, for example Anaglypta and contoured blown vinyls. Ceiling **ROSES**, **MOULDINGS** and **COVINGS** are also known as relief decoration.

REPRODUCTION Furniture, design and decoration materials made by modern methods and from modern materials to an original design from an earlier period. Older styles have been copied in this way since pre-Georgian times, and reproductions of reproductions are frequently found.

REVEAL The vertical side of a window or door opening, also called an embrasure.

ROSE A ceiling **RELIEF DECORATION**, which usually surrounds the central light fitting but may be positioned singly or in groups almost anywhere on the bed of the ceiling.

SCUMBLING A painting effect used to achieve a **WOOD GRAINING** or **MARBLING** effect. A scumble glaze is applied over a surface colour with a circular motion of the brush. Scumble glaze can be bought ready-made or mixed from artists' oil paint, linseed oil and turpentine.

SHADE A **HUE** which has been mixed with black or grey to deepen or soften it.

SKIRTING A border of wood or plaster which trims a wall where it meets the floor.

SPATTERING A decorative painted finish achieved by flicking or splashing colours over a solid colour ground. Different colours or different **VALUES** of a colour can be used together to create a soft, speckled effect.

SPECTRUM The colours of the rainbow - the pure hues of red, orange, yellow, green, blue and violet - which are created when white light is passed through a **PRISM**.

SPLIT-COMPLEMENTARY A colour **HARMONY** achieved with three colours - one pure **HUE** together with the two colours which appear on either side of its **COMPLEMENTARY** on a **COLOUR WHEEL**, for example green with red-orange and red-violet or blue with yellow-orange and red-orange.

SPONGING A painting technique used to create a soft texture, achieved by dabbing a top colour over a base coat with a natural sea sponge or artificial equivalent. A sponge can also be used to remove partially a still-wet top coat or **GLAZE**.

STIPPLING A painting technique which creates a slightly speckled texture. The tip of a stiff-bristled stippling or stencil brush is pounded on a wet surface or used to apply a second colour.

TINT A **HUE** which has been mixed with white to lighten it.

TONE A colour based on a **HUE**.

TONAL VALUE The gradation of one **HUE** from light to dark.

TENTING A method of draping a ceiling with fabric, sometimes continuing down the walls.

TROMPE L'OEIL The literal translation is eye-deceiver. Trompe l'oeil describes decorative illusions which deceive the eye, for example a sea view painted at the end of a corridor.

VALANCE A frill of fabric used to cover a bed base, or a frilled pelmet used to cover the top of a curtain.

VALUE A term used to describe the light or dark quality of a colour.

WOOD GRAINING The natural grain in timber, which can be simulated using painting techniques such as **COMBING** and **SCUMBLING**.

INDEX

ACKNOWLEDGEMENTS

The Publishers would like to thank the following for their assistance with this publication: Bisque Limited, Click Systems Limited, Cubic Metre Furniture, John Cullen Lighting Design, Lancelot Furniture, The London Sofa-Bed Centre, Nairn Floors Limited, Osborne and Little plc, Parkertex Fabrics Limited, Runtal Limited, Samhall UK Limited, The Sofa Bed Factory, Tiles Tiles Tiles. Architects and designers: Piers Gough, Richard Holly, Phillida Naess, Zandra Rhodes, Howard Allan, David Hodge, Michael Hopkins, Dinni and Julian Bendien, Alan Buchsbaum, David Rodes.

Quarto would also like to thank the following for permission to reproduce copyright material (Elizabeth Whiting and Associates is abbreviated to EWA): p.10 Home Improvements Guides; p.11 Home Improvements Guides; p.17 Tom Leighton, EWA; p.18 Michael Dunne, EWA; p.19 (top) Dulux ICI (bottom) Michael Dunne, EWA; p.21 (top) Michael Dunne (bottom) Tim Street-Porter, EWA; p.24 (top and bottom) Julian Niemain, EWA; p.25 (top and bottom) Home Beautiful; p.26 (left) Dennis Stone (right) Jerry Tubby, EWA; p.27 (top) Jerry Tubby (bottom) Neil Lorimer, EWA; p.28 Richard Davies, EWA; p.29 (top and bottom) Home Beautiful; p.30 Graham Henderson, EWA; p.31 (top) Jerry Tubby (bottom) Tim Street-Porter, EWA; p.32 (top) Michael Nicholson, EWA; p.35 Muraspec; p.38 Michael Nicholson, EWA; p.39 Home Beautiful; p.41 Michael Crockett, EWA; p.42 Stock Photos; p.46 Michael Dunne, EWA; p.47 Stock Photos; p.48 (top and bottom) Tom Leighton, EWA; p.51 Michael Dunne, EWA; p.54 Home Beautiful; p.55 (top) Stock Photos (bottom) Neil Lorimer, EWA; p.58 (left) EWA (right) Home Beautiful; p.59 Clive Itelm, EWA; p.62 Home Beautiful; p.63 Home Beautiful; p.65 (top) Tim Street-Porter, EWA (bottom) Home Beautiful; p.68 Home Beautiful; p.69 (left and top) Michael Nicholson, EWA (bottom) Home Beautiful; p.72 (top and bottom) Home Beautiful; p.73 Home Beautiful; p.76 Home Beautiful; p.77 (top) Friedhelm Thomas, (bottom) Michael Dunne, EWA; p.80 (top) Stock Photos (bottom) Home Beautiful; p.81 (top and bottom) Home Beautiful; p.84 Michael Nicholson, EWA; p.85 (top) Richard Davies, EWA (bottom) One-Off Limited; p.86 Michael Dunne, EWA; p.87 Cubic Metre Furniture; p.88 (top left, top right and bottom) Michael Dunne, EWA; p.89 (top) Michael Nicholson (bottom) Tim Street-Porter, EWA; p.92 Spike Powell, EWA; p.93 (top) Jerry Tubby (bottom) Michael Nicholson, EWA p.94 (top and bottom) Jerry Tubby, EWA; p.96 Jerry Tubby, EWA; p.100 Michael Dunne, EWA; p.101 John Cullen Lighting Design; p.102 Michael Dunne, EWA; p.116 Michael Dunne, EWA; p.117 Jerry Tubby, EWA; p.118 (top) Richard Davies, EWA; p.119 (bottom) Runtalrad Limited; p.120 Tom Leighton, EWA; p.122 (left) Tim Street Porter, EWA (right) Home Beautiful; p.123 (left) Michael Dunne, (right) Spike Powell, EWA; p.124 Jerry Tubby, EWA; p.125 (left) Lavinia Press (right) Michael Crockett, EWA; p.126 (top) Neil Lorimer (bottom) Tim Street-Porter, EWA; p.127 (top) Tim Street-Porter,EWA (bottom) Home Beautiful; p.129 (top and bottom) Michael Dunne, EWA; p. 131 Martex; p.132 Michael Dunne, EWA; p.133 Tim Street-Porter, EWA; p.137 Tim Street-Porter, EWA; p.140 Clive Helm, EWA; p.141 Neil Lorimer, EWA; p.142 (left and right) Gary Chowawitz, EWA; p.143 (left) Michael Dunne, EWA, (right) Stock Photos; p.144 (top) Amtico (middle and bottom) Tim Street-Porter, EWA; p.145 (left) Karen Bussolini (right) Dulux ICI; p.146 (left and right) Michael Dunne, EWA; p.147 (right) Spike Powell, (left) Home Beautiful; p.148 (left and right) Neil Lorimer, EWA; p.149 (top left and bottom) Home Beautiful (top right) Jerry Tubby, EWA, (centre) Tim Street-Porter, EWA; p.150 (top) Gary Chowawitz (bottom) Tim Street-Porter, EWA; p.151 Tim Street-Porter, EWA; p.152 Ron Sutherland, EWA; p.153 (top) Michael Dunne (bottom) Julian Nieman, EWA; p.154 (left)Tim Street-Porter (right) Friedhelm Thomas, EWA; p.155 David Lloyd, EWA; p.156 (left) Stock Photos; p.157 (left) Frank Interholdt (right) Friedhelm Thomas, EWA; p.160 (top) Design Council (bottom) Tim Street-Porter, EWA; p.161 (top) Home Beautiful (bottom right) Tim Street-Porter (bottom left) Spike Powell, EWA; p.162 (top) Michael Dunne, EWA (bottom) Home Beautiful; p.163 Home Beautiful; p.164 (top and bottom) Gary Chowawitz, EWA; p.165 (top) Christine Hanscomb (bottom left) Home Beautiful (bottom right) Jan Parrish, EWA; p.166 Jerry Tubby, EWA; p.167 (top) Michael Dunne (bottom left and bottom right) Neil Lorimer, EWA; p.168 (left) Christie's Colour Library (right) Giraudon; p.169 (left) Cassina Spa (right) Tim Street-Porter, EWA; p.170 (top and centre) Home Beautiful (bottom) Tim Street-Porter, EWA; p.171 (top, bottom left and bottom right) Home Beautiful (right) Arc Design; p.172 (top) Susan Shanks/Faber Blinds (bottom) Michael Nicholson, EWA; p.173 (top) Home Beautiful (bottom) Tim Street-Porter, EWA; p.174 (bottom right) Tim Street-Porter, EWA; p.175 (bottom) Tim Street-Porter, EWA All other photographs are the property of Quill Publishing Limited.

Every effort has been made to acknowledge all copyright holders and we would like to apologize if any omissions have been made.

Special thanks also to Carole Antoniou, Richard Bird, Judy Martin, Hilary Toovey and Susie Ward.